Donated
by
San Jose Mercury N
◁ S0-EGO-993

WITHDRAWN

808.8
TRE   Trees: a browser'
              s anthology
       c.1 $20.00

SAN BENITO COUNTY FREE LIBRARY
—————
Request for library materials
must be accompanied by bor-
rower's card. For overtime,
fines may vary, depending on
type of item checked out. No
library materials will be issued
to persons in arrears for fines.
For information call
(831) 636-4107.

WITHDRAWN

TREES

TREES

A BROWSER'S ANTHOLOGY

Selected and edited by

W. R. Martin

and

Warren U. Ober

P. D. Meany *Publishers*

Toronto

San Benito Co. Free Library
470 Fifth Street
Hollister, CA 95023

Every reasonable effort has been made to trace the owners of copyright material in this book, but in a few cases this has proven impossible. The publisher will be glad to receive information leading to more complete acknowledgments in subsequent printings of the book, and in the meantime extends apologies for any omissions or errors.

Selection and Critical Apparatus copyright © 1998 by
W. R. Martin and Warren U. Ober

Canadian Cataloguing in Publication Data

Main entry under title:

Trees : a browser's anthology

Includes index.
ISBN 0-88835-005-8

1. Trees – Literary collections. I. Martin, W. R. (Walter Rintoul), 1920–   . II. Ober, Warren U.

PN6071.T74T73 21998   808.8'0364   C98-930041-2

Jacket illustration is reproduced from the painting
Willows and Sumac by permission of the artist,
Wilfred Gelder of Streetsville, Ontario.

Jacket designed and typeset by Glen Patchet.
Text designed by Robin Brass Studio.

Printed on acid-free paper in Canada
for
P. D. Meany Publishers
Box 118, Streetsville
Ontario, Canada
L5M 2B7

Contents

Contents

Contents

Contents

Contents

Contents

⌒

List of Illustrations

TREES

A BROWSER'S ANTHOLOGY

Introduction

U NLESS WE LIVE in the Sahara, the Arctic, or perhaps the prairies we tend to take trees for granted. We are told our progenitors lived in them, and still today they loom around and above us and seem as immovable and permanent as the house we grow up in and the hills on the horizon. They are there to be climbed, to give us fruit for our delectation and wood for our fires. Then, as we grow older, they provide shelter and shade for our privacy and our daydreams, and, when we are older still, they become the objects of our thought, admiration, gratitude, and affection and even vehicles for philosophic reflection, religious sentiment, and poetic fervour. Although pioneers have thought of trees as nuisances or obstructions to be uprooted and cleared away for pasture and crops, now in the waning years of the twentieth century we have come to realize that trees are necessary for the health of our planet and for our survival on it.

Certainly the theme of trees has been a prominent feature in our lives ever since the Garden of Eden and has planted itself deep in the human consciousness. In metaphor and symbol trees provide endless metaphysical stimulus to the human spirit and imagination. The greenwood, whether in Eden, Arden, or Nottingham, has always been the setting of a joyous Golden Age. But the forest has also been the source of our oldest and deepest fears. Dante's journey to the Inferno begins as he loses his way in a dark wood, and every child knows about the big bad wolf. It is not only sheer terror that the jungle and its darkness bring to us; the unknown brings also awe. Thrilling mysteries invest the world of dryads and druids. Sir James G. Frazer's *The Golden Bough*, seminal for modern anthropology, starts in the sanctuary of Diana of the Woodland Glade at Nemi, and twentieth-century literary criticism begins with T.S. Eliot's *The Sacred Wood*. There are of course many reactions in between joy, on the one hand, and fear or awe, on the other, not least remarkable that of rest and relief, as conveyed in that fine poem by Edward Thomas, "Lights Out":

> I have come to the borders of sleep,
> The unfathomable deep
> Forest, where all must lose
> Their way....
> ....
> All pleasure and all trouble,
> Although most sweet or bitter,
> Here ends, in sleep that is sweeter
> Than tasks most noble.

The passages in this anthology exemplify some of the many aspects of trees as they appear to us in our lives, and, though we started collecting them simply for fun, after a time we felt that it would be appropriate to collect enough of various kinds to make an anthology that could have a place in the doctor's waiting room, in the glove compartment, and at the bedside. To give a title such as "literary arboretum" might imply pretentious suggestions of science and learning, whereas the object of this anthology is no more and no less than diversion and pleasure. It is, quite simply, a celebration of the infinitely rich and varied relationships between human beings and trees.

The chronological arrangement of the pieces will, we hope, be a convenience for those who have some framework of history in their minds, and it also brings home to us that trees have had a varied importance for us throughout the millennia of recorded history. One sign of this is that we have perhaps as many different names for trees as the Zulus have for cattle and the Inuit for snow: copse, holt, jungle, hanger, spinney, boscage, thicket, arboretum, orchard, chase, forest, rain-forest, plantation, grove, shaw, coppice, hurst, wood(s), woodland, wildwood, park, timber, bush, and so on, terms that have connotations ranging from pride and affection to mystery and fear.

There are many ways of reading an anthology. Perhaps the most common and the best way is merely to dart about at random, following one's eyes or fingers, to allow serendipity to produce its surprises and pleasures. But, for those who prefer formal order and plantations to natural wilderness and forests, we suggest, in the Appendix, some categories in which the passages might be grouped. Whichever method you prefer, we ask you to be tolerant and forgive us when you can't find your own favourite and indispensable passages. Instead of grousing, you might make your own anthology or, better still, let us know (care of our publisher) what additional selections we should include in the next edition.

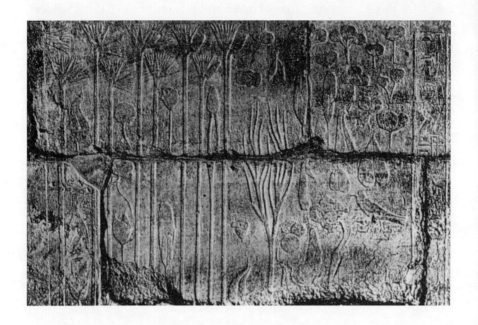

Plants brought to Egypt from Syria by Pharaoh Thutmose III. Limestone Relief.

From *Atlas Zur Altägyptischen Kulturgeschichte*, by Walter Wreszinski, Leipzig, 1923.

ca. 1450 B.C.

Gilgamesh

[The Cedar Mountain of the Gods]

They stood still and looked (?) at the forest.
They beheld the height of the cedar.
They beheld the entrance to the forest.
Where Humbaba was wont to walk there was a path;
Straight were the tracks and good was the passage.
They beheld the mountain of the cedar, the dwelling-place
Of the gods, the throne-dais of Irnini [probably a form of Ishtar].
The cedar uplifted its fulness before the mountain;
Fair was its shade (and) full of delight;
[Cov]ered was the brushwood (and) covered the [...].

Tablet V, column 1, translated by Alexander Heidel, 1946.
From *Gilgamesh, The Gilgamesh Epic And Old Testament Parallels*, translated by
Alexander Heidel, 2nd ed. Copyright 1949 by The University of Chicago Press.
Reprinted with permission.

ca. 2000 B.C.

The Bible

["A garden eastward in Eden"]

8   And the Lord God planted a garden eastward in Eden; and there he
     put the man whom he had formed.

9   And out of the ground made the Lord God to grow every tree that is
     pleasant to the sight, and good for food; the tree of life also in the
     midst of the garden, and the tree of knowledge of good and evil.

10   And a river went out of Eden to water the garden; and from thence it
     was parted, and became into four heads.

     ....

15 And the Lord God took the man, and put him into the garden of Eden to dress it and keep it.

16 And the Lord God commanded the man, saying, Of every tree of the garden thou mayest freely eat:

17 But of the tree of the knowledge of good and evil, thou shalt not eat of it: for in the day that thou eatest thereof thou shalt surely die.

From Genesis II, AV, 1611.

ca. 1000 B.C. (?)

⤿

Homer
[Menelaus kills Euphorbus]

Unmoved, Euphorbus thus: "That action known,
Come, for my brother's blood repay thy own.
....
No longer then defer the glorious strife,
Let heaven decide our fortune, fame, and life."
  Swift as the word the missile lance he flings;
The well-aim'd weapon on the buckler rings,
But blunted by the brass, innoxious falls.
On Jove the father great Atrides calls,
Nor flies the javelin from his arm in vain,
It pierced his throat, and bent him to the plain;
Wide through the neck appears the grisly wound,
Prone sinks the warrior, and his arms resound.
The shining circlets of his golden hair,
Which even the Graces might be proud to wear,
Instarr'd with gems and gold, bestrow the shore,
With dust dishonour'd, and deform'd with gore.
  As the young olive, in some sylvan scene,
Crown'd by fresh fountains with eternal green,

Lifts the gay head, in snowy flowerets fair,
And plays and dances to the gentle air;
When lo! a whirlwind from high heaven invades
The tender plant, and withers all its shades;
It lies uprooted from its genial bed,
A lovely ruin now defaced and dead:
Thus young, thus beautiful, Euphorbus lay,
While the fierce Spartan tore his arms away.

From *The Iliad*, XVII, translated by Alexander Pope, 1720.

ca. 900 B.C.

Homer

[Odysseus's olive-tree bedstead]

To him thus replied
The wise Penelope: "Man half-deified,
'Tis not my fashion to be taken straight
With bravest men, nor poorest used to sleight.
Your mean appearance made not me retire,
Nor this your rich show makes me now admire,
Nor moves at all; for what is all to me
If not my husband? All his certainty
I knew at parting; but, so long apart,
The outward likeness holds no full desert
For me to trust to. Go, nurse, see addrest
A soft bed for him, and the single rest
Himself affects so. Let it be the bed
That stands within our bridal chamber-sted,
Which he himself made. Bring it forth from thence,
And see it furnish'd with magnificence."
This said she to assay him, and did stir
Ev'n his establish'd patience; and to her

Whom thus he answer'd: "Woman! your words prove
My patience strangely. Who is it can move
My bed out of his place? It shall oppress
Earth's greatest understander; and, unless
Ev'n God himself come, that can eas'ly grace
Men in their most skills, it shall hold his place;
For man he lives not that (as not most skill'd,
So not most young) shall easily make it yield,
If, building on the strength in which he flows,
He adds both levers too and iron crows:
For in the fixture of the bed is shown
A master-piece, a wonder; and 'twas done
By me, and none but me, and thus was wrought:
There was an olive-tree that had his grought [growth]
Amidst a hedge, and was of shadow proud,
Fresh, and the prime age of his verdure show'd,
His leaves and arms so thick that to the eye
It show'd a column for solidity.
To this had I a comprehension
To build my bridal bow'r; which all of stone,
Thick as the tree of leaves, I rais'd, and cast
A roof about it nothing meanly grac'd,
Put glued doors to it, that op'd art enough.
Then from the olive ev'ry broad-leav'd bough
I lopp'd away; then fell'd the tree; and then
Went over it both with my axe and plane,
Both govern'd by my line. And then I hew'd
My curious bedstead out; in which I shew'd
Work of no common hand. All this begun,
I could not leave till to perfection
My pains had brought it; took my wimble, bor'd
The holes, as fitted, and did last afford
The varied ornament, which show'd no want
Of silver, gold, and polish'd elephant.
An ox-hide dyed in purple then I threw
Above the cords. And thus to curious view

I hope I have objected honest sign
To prove I author nought that is not mine.
But if my bed stand unremov'd or no,
O woman, passeth human wit to know."
This sunk her knees and heart, to hear so true
The signs she urg'd; and first did tears ensue
Her rapt assurance; then she ran and spread
Her arms about his neck, kiss'd oft his head.

From the *Odyssey*, XXIII, translated by George Chapman, 1615.

ca. 900 B.C.

᭝᭬

Hesiod

["Whet the sounding Ax to fell the Wood"]

When the hot Season of the Year is o'er
That draws the toilsome Sweat from ev'ry pore;
When o'er our Heads th' abated Planet rowls
A shorter Course, and visits distant Poles;
When *Jove* descends in Showrs upon the Plains,
And the parch'd Earth is cheer'd with plenteous Rains;
When human Bodys feel the grateful Change,
And less a Burden to themselves they range;
When the tall Forest sheds her Foliage round,
And with autumnal Verdure strews the Ground,
The Bole is incorrupt, the Timber good;
Then whet the sounding Ax to fell the Wood.
Provide a Mortar three Feet deep, and strong;
And let the Pistil be three Cubits long.
One Foot in Length next let the Mallet be;
Ten Spans the Wain, seven Feet her Axeltree,
Of Wood four crooked Bits the Wheel compose,

And give the Length three Spans to each of those.
  From Hill or Field the hardest Holm prepare,
To cut the Part in which you place the Share;
Thence your Advantage will be largely found,
With that your Oxen long may tear the Ground;
And next, the skilful Husbandman to show,
Fast pin the Handel to the Beam below:
Let the Draught-beam of sturdy Oak be made,
And for the Handel rob the Laurel Shade,
Or, if the Laurel you refuse to fell,
Seek out the Elm, the Elm will serve as well.

From *Works and Days*, II, translated by Thomas Cooke, 1728.

8th century B.C.

The Bible
[The Tree of Jesse]

X

30 Lift up thy voice, O daughter of Gallim: cause it to be heard unto Laish, O poor Anathoth.

31 Madmenah is removed; the inhabitants of Gebim gather themselves to flee.

32 As yet shall he remain at Nob that day: he shall shake his hand against the mount of the daughter of Zion, the hill of Jerusalem.

33 Behold, the Lord, the Lord of hosts, shall lop the bough with terror: and the high ones of stature shall be hewn down, and the haughty shall be humbled.

34 And he shall cut down the thickets of the forest with iron, and Lebanon shall fall by a mighty one.

"The Jesse Tree," British Library MS Lansdowne 383 (Shaftesbury Psalter).

Reproduced with the permission of The British Library. Ms Lansdowne 383.

1161-73

Lioness under a palm tree. Relief from the palace of Ashurbanipal,
King of Assyria.

Copyright The British Museum.

ca. 650 B.C.

XI

1 And there shall come forth a rod out of the stem of Jesse, and a Branch shall grow out of his roots:

2 And the spirit of the Lord shall rest upon him, the spirit of wisdom and understanding, the spirit of counsel and might, the spirit of knowledge and of the fear of the Lord;

3 And shall make him of quick understanding in the fear of the Lord: and he shall not judge after the sight of his eyes, neither reprove after the hearing of his ears:

4 But with righteousness shall he judge the poor, and reprove with equity for the meek of the earth: and he shall smite the earth with the rod of his mouth, and with the breath of his lips shall he slay the wicked.

5 And righteousness shall be the girdle of his loins, and faithfulness the girdle of his reins.

6 The wolf also shall dwell with the lamb, and the leopard shall lie down with the kid; and the calf and the young lion and the fatling together; and a little child shall lead them.

7 And the cow and the bear shall feed; their young ones shall lie down together: and the lion shall eat straw like the ox.

8 And the sucking child shall play on the hole of the asp, and the weaned child shall put his hand on the cockatrice' den.

9 They shall not hurt nor destroy in all my holy mountain: for the earth shall be full of the knowledge of the Lord, as the waters cover the sea.

10 And in that day there shall be a root of Jesse, which shall stand for an ensign of the people; to it shall the Gentiles seek: and his rest shall be glorious.

From Isaiah X & XI, AV, 1611.

ca. 711-701 B.C.

The Bible
["And he shall be like a tree"]

1 Blessed is the man that walketh not in the counsel of the ungodly, nor standeth in the way of sinners, nor sitteth in the seat of the scornful.

2 But his delight is in the law of the Lord; and in his law doth he meditate day and night.

3 And he shall be like a tree planted by the rivers of water, that bringeth forth his fruit in his season; his leaf also shall not wither; and whatsoever he doeth shall prosper.

4 The ungodly are not so: but are like the chaff which the wind driveth away.

5 Therefore the ungodly shall not stand in the judgment, nor sinners in the congregation of the righteous.

6 For the Lord knoweth the way of the righteous: but the way of the ungodly shall perish.

Psalm 1, AV, 1611.

ca. 7th century B.C.

The Bible
["Return, we beseech thee"]

7 Turn us again, O God of hosts, and cause thy face to shine; and we shall be saved.

8 Thou hast brought a vine out of Egypt: thou hast cast out the heathen, and planted it.

9 Thou preparedst room before it, and didst cause it to take deep root, and it filled the land.

10 The hills were covered with the shadow of it, and the boughs thereof were like the goodly cedars.

Psalm 1 ("And he shall be like a tree…") Utrecht Psalter. Ms 32, fol. 1v. (Detail).

Reproduced with the permission of Bibliotheek der Rijksuniversiteit te Utrecht.

ca. 820

11 She sent out her boughs unto the sea, and her branches unto the river.

12 Why hast thou then broken down her hedges, so that all they which pass by the way do pluck her?

13 The boar out of the wood doth waste it, and the wild beast of the field doth devour it.

14 Return, we beseech thee, O God of hosts: look down from heaven, and behold, and visit this vine:

15 And the vineyard which thy right hand hath planted, and the branch that thou madest strong for thyself.

16 It is burned with fire, it is cut down: they perish at the rebuke of thy countenance.

17 Let thy hand be upon the man of thy right hand, upon the son of man whom thou madest strong for thyself.

18 So will not we go back from thee: quicken us, and we will call upon thy name.

19 Turn us again, O Lord God of hosts, cause thy face to shine; and we shall be saved.

From Psalm 80, AV, 1611.

ca. 7th century B.C.

The Bible
[Graven Images]

9 They that make a graven image are all of them vanity; and their delectable things shall not profit; and they are their own witnesses; they see not, nor know; that they may be ashamed.

10 Who hath formed a god, or molten a graven image that is profitable for nothing?

11 Behold, all his fellows shall be ashamed: and the workmen, they are of men; let them all be gathered together, let them stand up; yet they shall fear, and they shall be ashamed together.

12 The smith with the tongs both worketh in the coals, and fashioneth it with hammers, and worketh it with the strength of his arms: yea, he is hungry, and his strength faileth: he drinketh no water, and is faint.

13 The carpenter stretcheth out his rule; he marketh it out with a line; he fitteth it with planes, and he marketh it out with the compass, and maketh it after the figure of a man, according to the beauty of a man; that it may remain in the house.

14 He heweth him down cedars, and taketh the cypress and the oak, which he strengtheneth for himself among the trees of the forest: he planteth an ash, and the rain doth nourish it.

15 Then shall it be for a man to burn: for he will take thereof, and warm himself; yea, he kindleth it, and baketh bread; yea, he maketh a god, and worshippeth it; he maketh it a graven image, and falleth down thereto.

16 He burneth part thereof in the fire; with part thereof he eateth flesh; he roasteth roast, and is satisfied: yea, he warmeth himself, and saith, Aha, I am warm, I have seen the fire:

17 And the residue thereof he maketh a god, even his graven image: he falleth down unto it, and worshippeth it, and prayeth unto it, and saith, Deliver me; for thou art my god.

18 They have not known nor understood: for he hath shut their eyes, that they cannot see; and their hearts, that they cannot understand.

19 And none considereth in his heart, neither is there knowledge nor understanding to say, I have burned part of it in the fire; yea, also I have baked bread upon the coals thereof; I have roasted flesh, and eaten it: and shall I make residue thereof an abomination? shall I fall down to the stock of a tree?

20 He feedeth on ashes: a deceived heart hath turned him aside, that he cannot deliver his soul, nor say, Is there not a lie in my right hand?

21 Remember these, O Jacob and Israel; for thou art my servant: I have formed thee; thou art my servant: O Israel, thou shalt not be forgotten of me.

From Isaiah XLIV, AV, 1611.

ca. 538 B.C.

~

W. B. Yeats
[The miracle-bred olive-tree]

Chorus. Come praise Colonus' horses, and come praise
    The wine-dark of the wood's intricacies,
    The nightingale that deafens daylight there,
    If daylight ever visit where,
    Unvisited by tempest or by sun,
    Immortal ladies tread the ground
    Dizzy with harmonious sound,
    Semele's lad a gay companion.

    And yonder in the gymnasts' garden thrives
    The self-sown self-begotten shape that gives
    Athenian intellect its mastery,
    Even the grey-leaved olive-tree
    Miracle-bred out of the living stone;
    Nor accident of peace nor war
    Shall wither that old marvel, for
    The great grey-eyed Athene stares thereon.

From "Colonus' Praise," 1928, translated from Sophocles' *Oedipus at Colonus.*
Reprinted with the permission of Simon & Schuster from *The Poems of W.B. Yeats:
A New Edition,* edited by Richard J. Finneran.
Copyright 1982 by Macmillan Publishing Company;
copyright renewed © 1956 by Georgie Yeats.

ca. 404 B.C.

✣

The Bible
[An orchard of pleasant fruits]

12 A garden inclosed is my sister, my spouse; a spring shut up, a fountain sealed.
13 Thy plants are an orchard of pomegranates, with pleasant fruits; camphire with spikenard,
14 Spikenard and saffron; calamus and cinnamon, with all trees of frankincense; myrrh and aloes, with all the chief spices:
15 A fountain of gardens, a well of living waters, and streams from Lebanon.
16 Awake, O north wind; and come, thou south; blow upon my garden, that the spices thereof may flow out. Let my beloved come into his garden, and eat his pleasant fruits.

From The Song of Solomon, IV, AV, 1611.

ca. 330 B.C.

✣

Marcus Tullius Cicero
["To plante & to sett trees"]

I leue to telle what delectacyon olde age takith in knowyng and considering the vertue & the naturell strength of alle thynges that be genderd on erthe / ffor of a smale grayne of a figge or of a litle smale pepyn or kernell of a roysyn or of a smale corne of whete or of ony othir seedys or of som smale wandes and braunchis the erthe engendreth grete tronkes and grete trees and bowes.

. . . .

And not olde men haue delectacyon of the trees that they sette / or that they doo to be sette, but also they deliten themsilf to sett a tree / & greffe it vpon anothir, which is the most subtile & most artificiall thyng that euir was founde by labourers of the londe.

·········

The seconde thought & solicitude of aged men is for to say that the
labourers will / that aftir the labourage of the feeldes be doon & sped /
Thenne that men put to laboure the curtilages of gardeyns for their herbage of herbys of dyuers colours & of dyuers complexions & in orchardes
makyng for to plante & to sett trees of fruytes bryngyng forth / as oyles
pomegarnades, orenges, figges dates / almandes, pomecedres, pechys, apples / perys, quynces medelers / chesteynes, & othir such fruytes of dyuers
kyndes / thies be goodys of kynde here aboue named & rehersed / whiche
come by the studye and diligent occupacyon of a good labourer in the
londe / a man may namely thenk, to become more riche and more delectable by that occupacyon / than by a besinesse or a werk which is
superfluyous vayne and ydill / That is to witt, by hawkyng fowlyng of
bryddes and huntyng of wilde bestis which belongith vnto yong men....

From *Tulle of Olde Age*, translated by William Caxton, 1481.

44 B.C.

Virgil
[Of Trees]

Not every land can nourish every tree.
Rivers are fringed with willows; alders grow
In thick morasses; rocky hills give birth
To barren mountain-ashes; myrtle-groves
Grow strongest by the shore; while Bacchus loves
An open eminence, and yews prefer
North winds and cold. Behold where men subdue
The very limits of the world, behold
The rude Gelonians in their paint, and homes
Of Eastern Arabs: to each tree its land.
Black ebony knows India alone,
Only Sabaeans grow the incense-bough.

Need I describe to thee the balsam-bole
Oozing sweet odours, and the berry fruit
Of ever-verdant thorn; or Ethiop groves
In woolly raiment soft and white, or how
The Chinese comb a silky fleece from leaves;
Or woods that hang o'er India's ocean waves,
The farthest corner of the world, whose trees
No arrow can o'ershoot, so high they soar?
. . . .
But neither Media's pageantry of woods,
Nor glorious Ganges, nay, nor Hermus' stream
Whose mud is gold, with Italy may vie.

Reprinted with the permission of J.M. Dent from *The Georgics*, II, in Virgil, *Eclogues And Georgics*, translated by Thomas Fletcher Royds, published by Everyman's Library, 1907; revised 1946.

ca. 33 B.C.

Ovid

[Phoebus Apollo and Daphne]

Now the first love of Phoebus was Daphne, daughter of Peneus, the river-god. It was no blind chance that gave this love, but the malicious wrath of Cupid. Delian Apollo, while still exulting over his conquest of the serpent, had seen him bending his bow with tight-drawn string, and had said: "What hast thou to do with the arms of men, thou wanton boy? That weapon befits my shoulders; for I have strength to give unerring wounds to the wild beasts, my foes, and have but now laid low the Python swollen with countless darts, covering whole acres with plague-engendering form. Do thou be content with thy torch to light the hidden fires of love, and lay not claim to my honours." And to him Venus' son replied: "Thy dart may pierce all things else, Apollo, but mine shall pierce thee; and by as much as all living things are less than deity, by so much less is thy glory than mine." So saying he shook his wings and, dashing upward through the air, quickly alighted on the shady peak of Parnasus. There he took from his quiver two darts of opposite effect: one puts to flight, the other kindles the flame of love. The one which kindles love is of gold and has a sharp, gleaming point; the other is blunt and tipped with lead. This last the god fixed in the heart of Peneus' daughter, but with the other he smote Apollo, piercing even unto the bones and marrow. Straightway he burned with love; but she fled the very name of love, rejoicing in the deep fastnesses of the woods, and in the spoils of beasts which she had snared, vying with the virgin Phoebe. A single fillet bound her locks all unarranged. Many sought her; but she, averse to all suitors, impatient of control and without thought for man, roamed the pathless woods, nor cared at all that Hymen, love, or wedlock might be. Often her father said: "Daughter, you owe me a son-in-law"; and often: "Daughter, you owe me grandsons." But she, hating the wedding torch as if it were a thing of evil, would blush rosy red over her fair face, and, clinging around her father's neck with coaxing arms, would say: "O father, dearest, grant me to enjoy perpetual virginity. Her father has already granted this to Diana." He, indeed, yielded to her request. But that beauty of thine, Daphne, forbade the fulfilment of thy desire, and thy form fitted not with thy prayer. Phoebus loves Daphne at sight, and longs to wed her; and what he longs for, that he hopes; and his own gifts of prophecy deceive him. And as the stubble of the harvested grain is kindled, as hedges burn with the torches which some traveller has chanced to put too near, or has gone off and left at break of day, so was the god consumed with flames, so did he burn in all his heart, and feed his fruitless love on hope. He looks at her hair hanging down her neck in disarray, and says: "What if it were arrayed?" He gazes at her eyes gleaming like stars, he gazes upon her lips, which but to gaze on does not satisfy. He marvels at her fingers, hands, and wrists, and her arms, bare to the shoulder; and what is hid he deems still lovelier. But she flees him swifter than the fleeting breeze, nor does she stop when he calls after her: "O nymph, O Peneus' daughter, stay! I who pursue thee am no enemy. Oh stay! So does the lamb flee from the wolf; the deer from the lion; so do doves on fluttering wing flee from the eagle; so every creature flees its foes. But love is the cause of my pursuit. Ah me! I fear that thou wilt fall, or brambles mar thy innocent limbs, and I be cause of pain to thee. The region here is rough through which thou hastenest. Run with less speed, I pray, and hold thy flight. I, too, will follow with less speed. Nay, stop and ask who thy lover is. I am no mountain-dweller, no shepherd I, no unkempt guardian here of flocks and herds. Thou knowest not, rash one, thou knowest not whom thou fleest, and for that reason dost thou flee. Mine is the Delphian land, and Claros, Tenedos, and the realm of Patara acknowledge me as lord. Jove is my father. By me what shall be, has been, and what is are all revealed; by me the lyre responds in harmony to song. My arrow is sure of aim, but oh, one arrow, surer than my own, has wounded my heart but now so fancy free. The art of medicine is my discovery. I am called Help-Bringer throughout the world, and all the potency of herbs is given unto me. Alas, that love is curable by no herbs, and the arts which heal all others cannot heal their lord!"

He would have said more, but the maiden pursued her frightened way and left him with his words unfinished, even in her desertion seeming fair. The winds bared her limbs, the opposing breezes set her garments a-flutter as she ran, and a light air flung her locks streaming behind her. Her beauty was enhanced by flight. But the chase drew to an end, for the youthful god would not longer waste his time in coaxing words, and urged on by love, he pursued at utmost speed. Just as when a Gallic hound has seen a hare in an open plain, and seeks his prey on flying feet, but the hare, safety; he, just about to fasten on her, now, even now thinks he has her, and grazes her very heels with his outstretched muzzle; but she knows not whether she be not already caught, and barely escapes from those sharp fangs and leaves behind the jaws just closing on her: so ran the god and maid, he sped by hope and she by fear. But he ran the more swiftly, borne on the wings of love, gave her no time to rest, hung over her fleeing shoulders and breathed on the hair that streamed over her neck. Now was her strength all gone, and, pale with fear and utterly overcome by the toil of her swift flight, seeing her father's waters near, she cried: "O father, help! if your waters hold divinity; change and destroy this beauty by which I pleased o'er well." Scarce had she thus prayed when a down-dragging numbness seized her limbs, and her soft sides were begirt with thin bark. Her hair was changed to leaves, her arms to branches. Her feet, but now so swift, grew fast in sluggish roots, and her head was now but a tree's top. Her gleaming beauty alone remained.

But even now in this new form Apollo loved her; and placing his hand upon the trunk, he felt the heart still fluttering beneath the bark. He embraced the branches as if human limbs, and pressed his lips upon the wood. But even the wood shrank from his kisses. And the god cried out to this: "Since thou canst not be my bride, thou shalt at least be my tree. My hair, my lyre, my quiver shall always be entwined with thee, O laurel. With thee shall Roman generals wreathe their heads, when shouts of joy shall acclaim their triumph, and long processions climb the Capitol. Thou at Augustus' portals shalt stand a trusty guardian, and keep watch over the civic crown of oak which hangs between. And as my head is ever young and my locks unshorn, so do thou keep the beauty of thy leaves perpetual." Paean was done. The laurel waved her new-made branches, and seemed to move her head-like top in full consent.

From *Metamorphoses*, I.
Reprinted by permission of the publishers and the Loeb Classical Library from
Ovid: Vol. III, *Metamorphoses*, translated by Frank J. Miller, Cambridge, Mass.:
Harvard University Press, 1916.

ca. 5 B.C.

ᚠᚫ

The Bible
["The true vine"]

1   I am the true vine, and my Father is the husbandman.

2   Every branch in me that beareth not fruit he taketh away: and every branch that beareth fruit, he purgeth it, that it may bring forth more fruit.

3   Now ye are clean through the word which I have spoken unto you.

4   Abide in me, and I in you. As the branch cannot bear fruit of itself, except it abide in the vine; no more can ye, except ye abide in me.

5   I am the vine, ye are the branches: He that abideth in me, and I in him, the same bringeth forth much fruit: for without me ye can do nothing.

6   If a man abide not in me, he is cast forth as a branch, and is withered; and men gather them, and cast them into the fire, and they are burned.

7   If ye abide in me, and my words abide in you, ye shall ask what ye will, and it shall be done unto you.

8   Herein is my Father glorified, that ye bear much fruit; so shall ye be my disciples.

9   As the Father hath loved me, so have I loved you: continue ye in my love.

10   If ye keep my commandments, ye shall abide in my love; even as I have kept my Father's commandments, and abide in his love.

From The Gospel according to St. John, XV, AV, 1611.

ca. 90 A.D.

ॐ

Plutarch
[Solon and the trees]

[Solon] appointed ... the spaces that should be kept and observed by those, that would set or plant trees in their ground, as being a man very skilfull in these matters. For he ordeined, that whosoever would plante any kynde of trees in his grounde, he should set them five foote a sonder one from another: but for the figge tree and olyve tree specially, that they should in any case be nine foote a sonder, bicause these two trees doe sp[r]ead out their branches farre of, and they cannot stand neere other trees, but they must needes hurte them very much. For besides that they drawe awaye the same that doth nourishe the other trees, they cast also a certaine moisture and steame upon them, that is very hurtefull and incommodious.

From *Lives of the Noble Grecians and Romanes*, translated by Sir Thomas North, 1579.

ca. 100 A.D.

St. Augustine
["How to possess a tree"]

For as he is better off, who knows how to possess a tree, and returns thanks to Thee for the use thereof, although he know not how many cubits high it is, or how wide it spreads, than he that can measure it, and count all its boughs, and neither owns it, nor knows or loves its Creator: so a believer, whose all this world of wealth is, and *who having nothing, yet possesseth all things*, by cleaving unto Thee, whom all things serve, though he know not even the circles of the Great Bear,…is in a better state than one who can measure the heavens, and number the stars, and poise the elements, yet neglecteth Thee *who hast made all things in number, weight, and measure.*

From *The Confessions of St. Augustine*, V, iv, translated by E.B. Pusey, 1907.

ca. 397 A.D.

Li Po
A Summer Day

Naked I lie in the green forest of summer….
Too lazy to wave my white feathered fan.
I hang my cap on a crag,
And bare my head to the wind that comes
Blowing through the pine trees.

From *The Works of Li Po, The Chinese Poet*, translated by Shigeyoshi Obata, 1922.

8th century

Beowulf

[Grendel's mere]

"My liege and king," went on the thane who led
the warriors in their hunt, "we then pursued
the monster's track through rocks, down wolf-slopes, past
the windy headlands till, at last, we came
abruptly to a mere, where all tracks ceased.
Over it hangs a grove, frost-covered, dense;
a waterfall, fen-grey and brackish, feeds
it from the north, and to the east, beneath
a pall of mist, the waters sink to hell.
Each night there burns upon the water there
a fearful flame; by day the sullen waves
slope up to meet the ashen sky, which weeps
to see the cursed spot. An antlered buck,
hard-pressed by slavering hounds, will rather die
there on the shore than plunge into the waves
or seek for shelter in the darkened grove –
so pleasant is that place, grim Grendel's mere.
And there, my liege, beneath those waves in some
ungodly cave must lurk the demon who,
last night, came here to work us woe, who seeks
to carry on the feud which Grendel had
with us, a feud we thought was finished now."
....
At daybreak next the warriors set out
along the trail of Grendel's dam; the king
rode forth in splendour, Beowulf astride
his jeweled steed beside him, and their troops
on either side. Over the steep rock slopes
they pressed, through narrow defiles, under crags,
and out upon the barren wasteland marked
with marsh and fen. Strange water beasts that lurked
in meres and on the rocky headlands heard

their martial horn and slunk away, enraged.
At length they reached the wannest mere of all,
the forest still with frost, the waterfall,
and at its foot the sullen, heaving waves.

Reprinted with the permission of W.K. Thomas from *Beowulf: A Paraphrase*,
by W.K. Thomas, *Revue de l'Université d'Ottawa* 37 (1967).

ca. 8th century

Anonymous
[The Cross Speaks]

Soldiers hacked me   from a hill in Judah:
they stripped me of my branches,   broke my trunk in two;
they strapped my upper part   across my upright base,
and made of me   a Roman mockery,
a wretched rood,   a cruel cross,
to hold their thieves,   vilest of men,
criminals scorned,   cursed on a cross.

By a refuse heap   they raised me high
between two other   twisted trees,
and there I beheld   the hero of men,
the lord of creation   led as a criminal,
the master of mankind   mocked by men;
he thrust himself towards me,   the tree of shame.
Pariah dogs,   they knew him there;
carrion birds,   they recognized him;
the earth itself   trembled, amazed;
but humans, his own,   they knew him not.

I wanted to bow,   but he nodded "No";
he clasped me in his arms,   embraced the tree.
"Lord," I pleaded,   "let me fall

28

and crush your enemies,   destroy your foes."
"Stand firm," he said;   "grow tall with me;
thrust me upward   upon my throne,
for I have come   to claim my own,
to gather them all   from upon my tree."

The humans pierced me   with their loathsome spikes,
arrows of hatred   tearing my flesh;
I shuddered sharp   with each hammer stroke,
but dared not strike back,   for he bade me hold.
I raised the King   of Heaven high;
I bore aloft   the body of God:
they reviled us both,   the blindest of men;
they knew not their crime: the Christ was on the cross!

Yet still I durst not   bend or fall,
even when drenched with blood   from my champion's side,
as the giver of life   languished in death.
All of creation,   except for men,
wept and bewailed   the death of our maker:
in darkness of dolor   we grieved and groaned.

At length, tired of their fun,   the taunters left;
to a faithful few   I yielded the corpse
and watched as they wrapped him   close in a cloth,
carved out a grave,   and laid him to rest,
lord of all victories,   limp in the tomb.
Dirgeful through dusk   they departed in pain,
leaving him there,   alone and bereft.

Silence descended   around us three,
as we went on weeping,   we crosses there,
we went on weeping   our burden's blood.

Reprinted with the permission of W.K. Thomas from "The Dream of the Rood,"
translated by W.K. Thomas, 1988.

ca. 8th century

"Tree of Virtue," Speculum Virginum. *Köln, Hist. Archiv der Stadt, Ms W 276 A.*

Reproduced with the permission of Rheinisches Bildarchiv, Köln.

1100-50

"Tree of Vice," Speculum Virginum. *Köln, Hist. Archiv der Stadt, Ms W 276 A.*

Reproduced with the permission of Rheinisches Bildarchiv, Köln.

1100-50

The Book of Taliesin
[The trees prepare for battle]

There is calling on Heaven,
And on Christ that he would effect
Their deliverance,
The all-powerful Lord.
If the Lord had answered,
Through charms and magic skill,
Assume the forms of the principal trees,
With you in array
Restrain the people
Inexperienced in battle.
When the trees were enchanted
There was hope for the trees,
That they should frustrate the intention
Of the surrounding fires....
Better are three in unison,
And enjoying themselves in a circle,
And one of them relating
The story of the deluge,
And of the cross of Christ,
And of the Day of Judgement near at hand.
The alder-trees in the first line,
They made the commencement.
Willow and quicken tree,
They were slow in their array.
The plum is a tree
Not beloved of men;
The medlar of a like nature,
Overcoming severe toil.
The bean bearing in its shade
An army of phantoms.
The raspberry makes

Not the best of food.
In shelter live,
The privet and the woodbine,
And the ivy in its season.
Great is the gorse in battle.
The cherry-tree had been reproached.
The birch, though very magnanimous,
Was late in arraying himself;
It was not through cowardice,
But on account of his great size.
The appearance of the...
Is that of a foreigner and a savage.
The pine-tree in the court,
Strong in battle,
By me greatly exalted
In the presence of kings,
The elm-trees are his subjects.
He turns not aside the measure of a foot,
But strikes right in the middle,
And at the farthest end.
The hazel is the judge,
His berries are thy dowry.
The privet is blessed.
Strong chiefs in war
Are the...and the mulberry.
Prosperous the beech-tree.
The holly dark green,
He was very courageous:
Defended with spikes on every side,
Wounding the hands.
The long-enduring poplars
Very much broken in fight.
The plundered fern;
The brooms with their offspring:
The furze was not well behaved
Until he was tamed.

The heath was giving consolation,
Comforting the people.
The black cherry-tree was pursuing.
The oak-tree swiftly moving,
Before him tremble heaven and earth,
Stout doorkeeper against the foe
Is his name in all lands.
The corn-cockle bound together,
Was given to be burnt.
Others were rejected
On account of the holes made
By great violence
In the field of battle.
Very wrathful the...
Cruel the gloomy ash.
Bashful the chestnut-tree,
Retreating from happiness.
There shall be a black darkness,
There shall be a shaking of the mountain,
There shall be a purifying furnace,
There shall first be a great wave,
And when the shout shall be heard –
Putting forth new leaves are the tops of the beech,
Changing form and being renewed from a withered
    state;
Entangled are the tops of the oak.

———————

From "The Battle of the Trees," translated by D.W. Nash, 1858.
Pre-13th century

Dante
[The Dark Wood]

In the midway of this our mortal life,
I found me in a gloomy wood, astray
Gone from the path direct: and e'en to tell,
It were no easy task, how savage wild
That forest, how robust and rough its growth,
Which to remember only, my dismay
Renews, in bitterness not far from death.
Yet, to discourse of what there good befel,
All else will I relate discover'd there.

　　How first I enter'd it I scarce can say,
Such sleepy dulness in that instant weigh'd
My senses down, when the true path I left....

From *The Divine Comedy*, "Hell," I, translated by H.F. Cary, 1806.
ca. 1315

Dante
[The Harpies' Forest]

Ere Nessus yet had reach'd the other bank,
We enter'd on a forest, where no track
Of steps had worn a way. Not verdant there
The foliage, but of dusky hue; not light
The boughs and tapering, but with knares deform'd
And matted thick: fruits there were none, but thorns
Instead, with venom fill'd. Less sharp than these,
Less intricate the brakes, wherein abide
Those animals, that hate the cultured fields,

Betwixt Corneto and Cecina's stream.
    Here the brute Harpies make their nest, the same
Who from the Strophades the Trojan band
Drove with dire boding of their future woe.
Broad are their pennons, of the human form
Their neck and countenance, arm'd with talons keen
The feet, and the huge belly fledged with wings.
These sit and wail on the drear mystic wood.
    The kind instructor in these words began:
"Ere farther thou proceed, know thou art now
I' th' second round, and shalt be, till thou come
Upon the horrid sand: look therefore well
Around thee, and such things thou shalt behold,
As would my speech discredit." On all sides
I heard sad plainings breathe, and none could see
From whom they might have issued. In amaze
Fast bound I stood. He, as it seem'd, believed
That I had thought so many voices came
From some amid those thickets close conceal'd,
And thus his speech resumed: "If thou lop off
A single twig from one of those ill plants,
The thought thou hast conceived shall vanish quite."
    Thereat a little stretching forth my hand,
From a great wilding gather'd I a branch,
And straight the trunk exclaim'd: "Why pluck'st me?"
Then, as the dark blood trickled down its side,
These words it added: "Wherefore tear'st me thus?
Is there no touch of mercy in thy breast?
Men once were we, that now are rooted here.
Thy hand might well have spared us, had we been
The souls of serpents." As a brand yet green,
That burning at one end from the other sends
A groaning sound, and hisses with the wind
That forces out its way, so burst at once
Forth from the broken splinter words and blood.
    I, letting fall the bough, remain'd as one

Assail'd by terror; and the sage replied:
"If he, O injured spirit! could have believed
What he hath seen but in my verse described,
He never against thee had stretch'd his hand.
But I, because the thing surpass'd belief,
Prompted him to this deed, which even now
Myself I rue. But tell him, who thou wast;
That for this wrong to do thee some amends,
In the upper world (for thither to return
Is granted him) thy fame he may revive."
"That pleasant word of thine," the trunk replied,
"Hath so inveigled me, that I from speech
Cannot refrain, wherein if I indulge
A little longer, in the snare detain'd,
Count it not grievous. I it was, who held
Both keys to Frederick's heart, and turn'd the wards,
Opening and shutting, with a skill so sweet,
That besides me, into his inmost breast
Scarce any other could admittance find.
The faith I bore to my high charge was such,
It cost me the life-blood that warm'd my veins."

<hr/>

From *The Divine Comedy*, "Hell," XIII, translated by H.F. Cary, 1806.

ca. 1315

Sir Gawain and the Green Knight
[Sir Gawain searches for the Green Chapel]

In the morning he rode merrily by a mountain, through a full deep and wondrous wild forest; high hills were on each side, and woods of huge and hoary oaks, a hundred of them together, beneath him. The hazel and the hawthorn were trailing together with rough, ragged moss spread on all sides. Sorrowful birds sang on the bare twigs and piped piteously through pain of the cold. Upon Gringolet the man glided underneath them, all alone, through mud and mire, careful of his labour, lest he should be too late to see the service of his Lord, who on that night was born of a maiden our strife to be ending. Therefore, sighing, he said, 'I beseech thee, O Lord, and Mary, our dearest and mildest mother, that ye would grant me some place of rest where I might hear the Mass and matins of this moon. Full meekly I ask it, and thereto I will say full soon my pater and ave

and creed.'
He rode as he prayed,
And cried for misdeed,
And sign of Cross made,
And said, 'Christ's Cross me speed.'

Scarcely had he thrice signed himself with the sign of the Cross, when he was ware of a castle in the wood, on an upland or hill embosomed in the foliage of many a burly monarch of the forest. It was the comeliest castle that ever a knight possessed, in the centre of a meadow, with a park all about it. A palace beautiful, and for more than two miles encircled by trees. The knight caught sight of this palace of refuge on one side, shimmering and shining through the sheeny oaks. He gently doffed his helmet, and gave high thanks to Jesus and St. Gilyan, who had both of them gently and courteously guided his footsteps and hearkened to his crying. 'Now,' quoth the knight, 'grant me good hostel.' When putting his gilt heels to Gringolet, fully by chance he chose the right path, and full soon it brought him to the end of the drawbridge

at last.
The bridge was soon upraised,
The gates were shut so fast,
The walls were well appraised,
They feared not the wind's blast.

From *Sir Gawain And The Green Knight*, translated by Ernest J.B. Kirtlan,
Charles H. Kelly, Publishers, London, 1912.

ca. 1375–1400

Geoffrey Chaucer

["I shal thee showen mater of to wryte"]

With that my hond in his he took anoon,
Of which I comfort caughte, and wente in faste;
But lord! so I was glad and wel begoon!
For over-al, wher that I myn eyen caste,
Were treës clad with leves that ay shal laste,
Eche in his kinde, of colour fresh and grene
As emeraude, that joye was to sene.

The bilder ook, and eek the hardy asshe;
The piler elm, the cofre unto careyne;
The boxtree piper; holm to whippes lasshe;
The sayling firr; the cipres, deth to pleyne;
The sheter ew, the asp for shaftes pleyne;
The olyve of pees, and eek the drunken vyne,
The victor palm, the laurer to devyne.

A garden saw I, ful of blosmy bowes,
Upon a river, in a grene mede,
Ther as that swetnesse evermore y-now is,
With floures whyte, blewe, yelowe, and rede;
And colde welle-stremes, no-thing dede,
That swommen ful of smale fisshes lighte,
With finnes rede and scales silver-brighte.

On every bough the briddes herde I singe,
With voys of aungel in hir armonye,
Som besyed hem hir briddes forth to bringe;
The litel conyes to hir pley gunne hye,
And further al aboute I gan espye
The dredful roo, the buk, the hert and hinde,
Squerels, and bestes smale of gentil kinde.

[Birds, with trees]. Woodcut for Geoffrey Chaucer's The Parlement of Fowles.

ca. 1526

Of instruments of strenges in acord
Herde I so pleye a ravisshing swetnesse,
That god, that maker is of al and lord,
Ne herde never better, as I gesse;
Therwith a wind, unnethe hit might be lesse,
Made in the leves grene a noise softe
Acordant to the foules songe on-lofte.

The air of that place so attempre was
That never was grevaunce of hoot ne cold;
Ther wex eek every holsom spyce and gras,
Ne no man may ther wexe seek ne old;
Yet was ther joye more a thousand fold
Then man can telle; ne never wolde it nighte,
But ay cleer day to any mannes sighte.

From *The Parlement of Fowles.*

ca. 1380

Geoffrey Chaucer
[Prince Arcite's funeral pyre]

Heigh labour, and ful greet apparaillinge
Was at the service and the fyr-makinge,
That with his grene top the heven raughte,
And twenty fadme of brede the armes straughte;
This is to seyn, the bowes were so brode.
Of stree first ther was leyd ful many a lode.
But how the fyr was maked up on highte,
And eek the names how the treës highte,
As ook, firre, birch, asp, alder, holm, popler,
Wilow, elm, plane, ash, box, chasteyn, lind, laurer,

Mapul, thorn, beech, hasel, ew, whippel-tree,
How they weren feld, shal nat be told for me;
Ne how the goddes ronnen up and doun,
Disherited of hir habitacioun,
In which they woneden in reste and pees,
Nymphes, Faunes, and Amadrides;
Ne how the bestes and the briddes alle
Fledden for fere, whan the wode was falle;
Ne how the ground agast was of the light,
That was nat wont to seen the sonne bright;
Ne how the fyr was couched first with stree,
And than with drye stokkes cloven a three,
And than with grene wode and spycerye,
And than with cloth of gold and with perrye,
And gerlandes hanging with ful many a flour,
The mirre, th'encens, with al so greet odour;
Ne how Arcite lay among al this,
Ne what richesse aboute his body is.

From "The Knightes Tale" in *The Canterbury Tales*.

ca. 1390

St. Christopher, with a palm-tree staff. Woodcut.

1423

[Newborn babe in group, with trees]. Woodcut for *Sir Thomas Malory's*
Le Morte Darthur.

1498

❧

Anonymous
["Under the grene-wode tre"]

In somer, when the shawes be sheyne,
    And leves be large and long,
Hit is full mery in feyre foreste
    To here the foulys song:

To se the dere draw to the dale,
    And leve the hillès hee,
And shadow hem in the levës grene,
    Under the grene-wode tre.

———————

From "Robin Hood and the Monk."

ca. 1450

❧

Anonymous
[In the greenwood]

When shaws beene sheene, and shradds full fayre,
    And leves both large and longe,
Itt is merrye walking in the fayre forrèst
    To heare the small birds' songe.

The woodweele sang, and wold not cease,
    [Sitting upon the spraye,
Soe lowde, he wakened Robin Hood,
    In the grenewood where he lay.

"Now by my faye," sayd jollye Robin,
"A sweaven I had this night;
I dreamt me of two wight yemen,
That fast with me can fight."]

From "Robin Hood and Guy of Gisborne."
ca. 15th century

Anonymous
[How Mark lost Isolt to Tristan]

And then peace was made by Arthur between Trystan and March y Meirchion, and Arthur conversed with the two of them in turn, and neither of them was willing to be without Esyllt. Then Arthur adjudged her to one while the leaves should be on the wood, and to the other during the time that the leaves should not be on the wood, the husband to have the choice. And the latter chose the time when the leaves should not be on the wood, because the night is longest during that season. And Arthur announced that to Esyllt, and she said, "Blessed be the judgment and he who gave it!" And Esyllt sang this *englyn*:

"Three trees are good in nature:
the holly, the ivy, and the yew,
which keep their leaves throughout their lives;
I am Trystan's as long as he lives!"

And in this way March y Meirchion lost his wife forever. And so ends the story.

From "A Welsh Tristan Episode," translated by Tom Peete Cross, in
Studies in Philology, 17, 1920, University of North Carolina Press.

ca. 1550

[Hermit and devils, with chapel and trees]. Woodcut for
Richard Rolle's Contemplacyons.

1506

§

William Harrison

["Blessings from the most high God"]

And even as it fareth with our gardens, so doth it with our orchards, which were never furnished with so good fruit nor with such variety as at this present. For, beside that we have most delicate apples, plums, pears, walnuts, filberts, etc., and those of sundry sorts, planted within forty years past, in comparison of which most of the old trees are nothing worth, so have we no less store of strange fruit, as apricots, almonds, peaches, figs, corn-trees in noblemen's orchards. I have seen capers, oranges and lemons, and heard of wild olives growing here, beside other strange trees brought from far, whose names I know not. So that England for these commodities was never better furnished, neither any nation under their clime more plentifully endued with these and other blessings from the most high God, who grant us grace withal to use the same to his honour and glory, and not as instruments and provocations unto further excess and vanity, wherewith his displeasure may be kindled, lest these his benefits do turn unto thorns and briers unto us for our annoyance and punishment, which he hath bestowed upon us for our consolation and comfort.

From *Description of England*, modernized by J. Dover Wilson, 1913, for *Life in Shakespeare's England*, Cambridge University Press, 1913.

1587

Edmund Spenser

[Wandering to and fro in ways unknown]

And foorth they passe, with pleasure forward led,
    Joying to heare the birdes sweete harmony,
    Which therein shrouded from the tempest dred,
    Seemd in their song to scorne the cruell sky.
    Much can they prayse the trees, so straight and hy,
    The sayling Pine, the Cedar proud and tall,
    The vine-prop Elme, the Poplar never dry,
    The builder Oake, sole king of forrests all,
The Aspine good for staves, the Cypresse funerall.

The Laurell, meed of mightie Conquerours
    And Poets sage, the Firre that weepeth still,
    The Willow worne of forlorne Paramours,
    The Eugh obedient to the benders will,
    The Birch for shaftes, the Sallow for the mill,
    The Mirrhe sweete bleeding in the bitter wound,
    The warlike Beech, the Ash for nothing ill,
    The fruitfull Olive, and the Platane round,
The carver Holme, the Maple seeldom inward sound.

Led with delight, they thus beguile the way,
    Untill the blustring storme is overblowne;
    When weening to returne, whence they did stray,
    They cannot finde that path, which first was showne,
    But wander too and fro in wayes unknowne,
    Furthest from end then, when they neerest weene,
    That makes them doubt, their wits be not their owne:
    So many pathes, so many turnings seene,
That which of them to take, in diverse doubt they been.

From *The Faerie Queene*, I, i.

1589

49

ℱᴲ

Thomas Nashe

[Rome]

To tell you of the rare pleasures of their gardens, theyr bathes, theyr vineyardes, theyr galleries, were to write a seconde part of the gorgeous Gallerie of gallant devices. Why, you should not come into anie mannes house of account, but hee hadde fish-pondes and little orchardes on the toppe of his leads.... I sawe a summer banketting house belonging to a merchaunt, that was the mervaile of the world, and could not be matcht except God should make another paradise. It was builte round of greene marble, like a Theater with-out: within there was a heaven and earth comprehended both under one roofe, the heaven was a cleere overhanging vault of christall, wherein the Sunne and Moone, and each visible Starre had his true similitude, shine, scituation, and motion, and by what enwrapped arte I cannot conceive, these spheares in their proper orbes observed their circular wheelinges and turnings, making a certaine kinde of soft angelical murmering musicke in their often windings and going about, which musick the philosophers say in the true heaven by reason of the grosenes of our senses we are not capable of. For the earth it was counterfeited in that liknes that Adam lorded out it before his fall. A wide vast spacious roome it was, such as we would conceit prince Arthurs hall to be, where he feasted all his knights of the round table together everie penticost. The flore was painted with the beautifullest flowers that ever mans eie admired which so linealy were delineated, that he that viewd them a farre off and had not directly stood poaringly over them, would have sworne they had lived in deede. The wals round about were hedgde with Olives and palme trees, and all other odoriferous fruit-bearing plants, which at anie solemne intertainment dropt mirrhe and frankensence. Other trees that bare no fruit, were set in just order one against another, and divided the roome into a number of shadie lanes, leaving but one over spreading pine tree arbor, where wee sate and banketted. On the wel clothed boughs of this conspiracie of pine trees against the resembled Sun beames, were pearcht as many sortes of shrill breasted birdes as the Summer hath allowed for singing men in hir silvane chappels. Who though there were bodies without soules, and sweete resembled substances without sense, yet by the mathematicall experimentes of long silver pipes secretlye inrinded in the intrailes of the boughs whereon they sate, and undiscerneablie convaid under their bellies into their small throats sloaping, they whistled and freely carold theyr naturall field note. Neyther went those silver pipes straight, but by many edged unsundred writhings, and crankled wanderinges aside strayed from bough to bough into an hundred throats. But into this silver pipe so writhed and wandering aside, if anie demand how the wind was breathed; Forsoth the tail of the silver pipe stretcht it selfe into the mouth of a great paire of belowes, where it was close soldered, and bailde a bout with yron, it coulde not stirre or have anie vent betwixt. Those bellowes with the rising and falling of leaden plummets wounde up on a wheele, dyd beate up and downe uncessantly, and so gathered in wind, serving with one blast all the snarled pipes to and fro of one tree at once. But so closely were all those organising implements obscured in the corpulent trunks of the trees, that everie man there present renounst conjectures of art, and sayd it was done by inchantment.

From *The Unfortunate Traveller.*

1594

ৎ৯

William Shakespeare

[Husbandry, horticultural and political]

Queen. But stay, here come the gardeners:
Let's step into the shadow of these trees.
My wretchedness unto a row of pins,
They'll talk of state; for every one doth so
Against a change; woe is forerun with woe.
                              Queen and Ladies step aside.
Gard. Go, bind thou up yon dangling apricocks,
Which, like unruly children, make their sire
Stoop with oppression of their prodigal weight:
Give some supportance to the bending twigs.
Go thou, and like an executioner,
Cut off the heads of too fast growing sprays,
That look too lofty in our commonwealth:
All must be even in our government.
You thus employ'd, I will go root away
The noisome weeds, which without profit suck
The soil's fertility from wholesome flowers.
Serv. Why should we in the compass of a pale
Keep law and form and due proportion,
Showing, as in a model, our firm estate,
When our sea-walled garden, the whole land,
Is full of weeds; her fairest flowers chok'd up,
Her fruit-trees all unprun'd, her hedges ruin'd,
Her knots disorder'd, and her wholesome herbs
Swarming with caterpillars?
Gard.   Hold thy peace:
He that hath suffer'd this disorder'd spring
Hath now himself met with the fall of leaf:
The weeds which his broad-spreading leaves did shelter,
That seem'd in eating him to hold him up,
Are pluck'd up root and all by Bolingbroke;

52

I mean the Earl of Wiltshire, Bushy, Green.
Serv. What, are they dead?
Gard.   They are; and Bolingbroke
   Hath seized the wasteful king. O! what pity is it
   That he had not so trimm'd and dress'd his land
   As we this garden! We at time of year
   Do wound the bark, the skin of our fruit-trees,
   Lest, being over-proud in sap and blood,
   With too much riches it confound itself:
   Had he done so to great and growing men,
   They might have liv'd to bear and he to taste
   Their fruits of duty; superfluous branches
   We lop away, that bearing boughs may live:
   Had he done so, himself had borne the crown,
   Which waste of idle hours hath quite thrown down.

From *Richard II*, III, iv.

1597

❦

Anonymous

["My little nut tree"]

I had a little nut tree,
   Nothing would it bear
But a silver nutmeg
   And a golden pear;
The King of Spain's daughter
   Came to visit me,
And all for the sake
   Of my little nut tree.

Mother Goose rhyme.

16th or 17th century

✣

William Shakespeare
["Sweet are the uses of adversity"]

The Forest of Arden.
Enter Duke senior, Amiens, and two or
three Lords, like foresters.

Duke senior. Now, my co-mates, and brothers in exile,
Hath not old custom made this life more sweet
Than that of painted pomp? Are not these woods
More free from peril than the envious court?
Here feel we but the penalty of Adam,
The season's difference; as the icy fang
And churlish chiding of the winter's wind,
Which, when it bites and blows upon my body,
Even till I shrink with cold, I smile, and say
'This is no flattery: these are counsellors
That feelingly persuade me what I am.'
Sweet are the uses of adversity,
Which, like the toad, ugly and venomous,
Wears yet a precious jewel in his head:
And this our life, exempt from public haunt,
Finds tongues in trees, books in the running brooks,
Sermons in stones, and good in everything.
I would not change it.

————

From *As You Like It*, II, 1.

1600

✆

William Shakespeare
[The wood that moved]

Siward What wood is this before us?
Menteith   The wood of Birnam.
Malcolm Let every soldier hew him down a bough,
　　And bear't before him: thereby shall we shadow
　　The numbers of our host, and make discovery
　　Err in report of us.
Soldiers   It shall be done.

. . . .

Messenger Gracious my lord,
　　I should report that which I say I saw,
　　But know not how to do it.
Macbeth   Well, say, sir.
Mess. As I did stand my watch upon the hill,
　　I look'd toward Birnam, and anon, methought,
　　The wood began to move.
Macb.   Liar and slave!
Mess. Let me endure your wrath, if't be not so:
　　Within this three mile may you see it coming;
　　I say, a moving grove.
Macb.   If thou speak'st false,
　　Upon the next tree shalt thou hang alive,
　　Till famine cling thee: if thy speech be sooth,
　　I care not if thou dost for me as much.
　　I pull in resolution, and begin
　　To doubt th' equivocation of the fiend
　　That lies like truth: 'Fear not, till Birnam wood
　　Do come to Dunsinane;' and now a wood
　　Comes toward Dunsinane. Arm, arm, and out!

―――――――

From *Macbeth*, V, iv and v.

1606

ℰ

William Shakespeare

["We must not rend our subjects from our laws"]

Wolsey   If we shall stand still,
In fear our motion will be mocked or carped at,
We should take root here where we sit, or sit
State-statues only.
King   Things done well,
And with a care, exempt themselves from fear;
Things done without example, in their issue
Are to be feared. Have you a precedent
Of this commission? I believe, not any.
We must not rend our subjects from our laws
And stick them in our will. Sixth part of each?
A trembling contribution! why, we take
From every tree lop, bark, and part o' th' timber,
And though we leave it with a root, thus hacked,
The air will drink the sap. To every county
Where this is questioned, send our letters with
Free pardon to each man that has denied
The force of this commission. Pray look to 't;
I put it to your care.

From *King Henry VIII*, I, ii

1613

&

George Wither
[The Palm]

This is that fruitfull *Plant*, which when it growes,
Where wholesome *Water* in abundance flowes,
Was, by the *Psalmist*, thought a likely *Tree*,
The *Emblem*, of a *blessed-man*, to bee:
For, many wayes, it fitly typifies,
The *Righteous-man*, with his proprieties;
And, those true *Vertues*, which doe helpe increase
His growing, in the state of *Blessednesse*.

The *Palme*, (in this our *Emblem*, figur'd, thus)
Depressed with a *Stone*, doth shew to us
The pow'r of *Truth*: For, as this *Tree* doth spread,
And thrive the more, when weights presse downe the head;
So, *Gods* eternall *Truth* (which all the pow'r
And spight of *Hell*, did labour to devoure)
Sprung high, and flourished the more, thereby,
When *Tyrants* crush'd it, with their crueltie.
And, all inferiour *Truths*, the same will doe,
According as they make approaches to
The best *Perfection*; or, as they conduce
To *God's* due *praise*, or some such pious use.

Lord, still, preserve this *Truth's* integritie,
Although on ev'ry side, the wicked prie,
To spie how they may disadvantage it.
Yea, *Lord*, though *Sinners* in high place doe sit,
(As *David* saith) yet, let them not oppresse
Thy *Veritie*, by their imperiousnesse.
But, make both *Her*, and her *Professors*, bide
The *Test*, like *Silver* seven times purifide.

That, all *Truths* lovers, may with comfort see,
Shee may *deprest*, but, not, *oppressed* bee.

From *A Collection of Emblemes, Ancient and Moderne*, III.

1635

George Wither, "The Palm." From A Collection of Emblemes, Ancient and Moderne, *III.*

1635

Andrew Marvell
[Within the forest]

When first the eye this forest sees
It seems indeed as wood not trees:
As if their neighborhood so old
To one great trunk them all did mold.
There the huge bulk takes place, as meant
To thrust up a fifth element;
And stretches still so closely wedged
As if the night within were hedged.

Dark all without it knits; within
It opens passable and thin:
And in as loose an order grows
As the Corinthian porticoes.
The arching boughs unite between
The columns of the temple green;
And underneath the wingëd choirs
Echo about their tunëd fires.

The nightingale does here make choice
To sing the trials of her voice.
Low shrubs she sits in, and adorns
With music high the squatted thorns.
But highest oaks stoop down to hear,
And list'ning elders prick the ear.
The thorn, lest it should hurt her, draws
Within the skin its shrunken claws.

But I have for my music found
A sadder, yet more pleasing sound:
The stock doves, whose fair necks are graced
With nuptial rings, their ensigns chaste;
Yet always, for some cause unknown,
Sad pair, unto the elms they moan.
O why should such a couple mourn,
That in so equal flames do burn!

Then as I careless on the bed
Of gelid strawberries do tread,
And through the hazels thick espy
The hatching throstle's shining eye,
The heron from the ash's top
The eldest of its young lets drop,
As if it, stork-like, did pretend
That tribute to its Lord to send.

But most the hewel's wonders are,
Who here has the *holt-felster's* care.
He walks still upright from the root,
Meas'ring the timber with his foot;
And all the way, to keep it clean,
Doth from the bark the wood-moths glean.
He, with his beak, examines well
Which fit to stand and which to fell.

The good he numbers up, and hacks;
As if he marked them with the ax.
But where he, tinkling with his beak,
Does find the hollow oak to speak,
That for his building he designs,
And through the tainted side he mines.
Who could have thought the tallest oak
Should fall by such a feeble stroke!

Nor would it, had the tree not fed
A traitor worm, within it bred.
(As first our flesh corrupt within
Tempts impotent and bashful sin.)
And yet that worm triumphs not long,
But serves to feed the hewel's young:
While the oak seems to fall content,
Viewing the treason's punishment.

Thus I, easy philosopher,
Among the birds and trees confer:
And little now to make me, wants,
Or of the fowls or of the plants.
Give me but wings as they, and I
Straight floating on the air shall fly:
Or turn me but, and you shall see
I was but an inverted tree.

From "Upon Appleton House."

ca. 1653

Henry Vaughan

From "The Timber"

Sure thou didst flourish once! and many springs,
Many bright mornings, much dew, many showers
Passed o'er thy head: many light hearts and wings
Which now are dead, lodged in thy living bowers.

And still a new succession sings and flies;
Fresh groves grow up, and their green branches shoot
Towards the old and still enduring skies,
While the low violet thrives at their root.

But thou beneath the sad and heavy line
Of death, doth waste all senseless, cold, and dark;
Where not so much as dreams of light may shine,
Nor any thought of greenness, leaf or bark.

And yet (as if some deep hate and dissent,
Bred in thy growth betwixt high winds and thee,
Were still alive) thou dost great storms resent
Before they come, and know'st how near they be.

Else all at rest thou liest, and the fierce breath
Of tempests can no more disturb thy ease;
But this thy strange resentment after death
Means only those, who broke (in life) thy peace.

So murdered man, when lovely life is done,
And his blood freezed, keeps in the centre still
Some secret sense, which makes the dead blood run
At his approach that did the body kill.

And is there any murderer worse than sin?
Or any storms more foul than a lewd life?
Or what resentient can work more within,
Than true remorse, when with past sins at strife?

1655

Samuel Pepys
[A tree that righted itself]

25th [Feb]. The great talk was of the effects of this late great wind; and I heard one say that he had five great trees standing together blown down; and, beginning to lop them, one of them, as soon as the lops were cut off, did, by the weight of the root, rise again and fasten. We have letters from the forest of Deane, that above 1000 oakes and as many beeches are blown down in one walk there. And letters from my father tell me of £20 hurt done to us at Brampton.

From *The Diary of Samuel Pepys.*
1662

Samuel Pepys
[Bee-keeping in a Baltic Country]

11th [Dec]. They tell us that beares there do never hurt any body, but fly away from you, unless you pursue and set upon them; but wolves do much mischief. Mr. Harrington told us how they do to get so much honey as they send abroad. They make hollow a great fir-tree, leaving only a small slit down straight in one place, and this they close up again, only leave a little hole, and there the bees go in and fill the bodys of those trees as full of wax and honey as they can hold; and the inhabitants at times go and open the slit, and take what they please without killing the bees, and so let them live there still and make more. Fir trees are always planted close together, because of keeping one another from the violence of the windes; and when a fell is made, they leave here and there a grown tree to preserve the young ones coming up.

From *The Diary of Samuel Pepys.*
1663

❨

Samuel Pepys

["Lord! to see how we poor wretches dare not do the King good
service for fear of the greatness of these men."]

14th [July]. [Lord Sandwich] told me what a misfortune was fallen upon
me and him: on me, by a displeasure which my Lord Chancellor
[Clarendon] did show to him last night against me, in the highest and
most passionate manner that ever any man did speak, even to the not
hearing of any thing to be said to him.... And what should the business
be, but that I should be forward to have the trees in Clarendon Park
marked and cut down, which he, it seems, hath bought of my Lord
Albemarle; when, God knows! I am the most innocent man in the world
in it, and did nothing of myself, nor knew of his concernment therein,
but barely obeyed my Lord Treasurer's warrant for the doing thereof....
So... I to my Lord Chancellor's; and there, coming out after dinner, I ac-
costed him, telling him that I was the unhappy Pepys that had fallen into
his high displeasure, and come to desire him to give me leave to make
myself better understood to his Lordship.... He answered me very pleas-
ingly, that he was confident upon the score of my Lord Sandwich's character of me, but that he had reason to think what he did, and desired me
to call upon him some evening: I named tonight, and he accepted of it....
After all done, he himself called, "Come, Mr. Pepys, you and I will take a
turn in the garden." So he was led down stairs, having the goute, and there
walked with me, I think, above an hour, talking most friendly, yet cun-
ningly.... I think I did thoroughly appease him, till he thanked me for my
desire and pains to satisfy him; and, upon my desiring to be directed who
I should of his servants advise with about this business, he told me no-
body, but would be glad to hear from me himself. He told me he would
not direct me in any thing, that it might not be said that the Lord Chancellor did labour to abuse the King.... He did plainly say that he would
not direct me in any thing, for he would not put himself into the power
of any man to say that he did so and so; but plainly told me as if he would

be glad I did something. Lord! to see how we poor wretches dare not to do the King good service for fear of the greatness of these men.

From *The Diary of Samuel Pepys.*

1664

John Milton
[A view of Eden]

 So on he fares, and to the border comes
Of Eden, where delicious Paradise,
Now nearer, crowns with her enclosure green,
As with a rural mound, the champain head
Of a steep wilderness, whose hairy sides
With thicket overgrown, grotesque and wild,
Access denied; and overhead up grew
Insuperable highth of loftiest shade,
Cedar, and pine, and fir, and branching palm,
A sylvan scene, and, as the ranks ascend
Shade above shade, a woody theatre
Of stateliest view. Yet higher than their tops
The verdurous wall of Paradise up sprung;
Which to our general sire gave prospect large
Into his nether empire neighbouring round.
And higher than that wall a circling row
Of goodliest trees, loaden with fairest fruit,
Blossoms and fruits at once of golden hue,
Appear'd, with gay enamell'd colours mix'd;
On which the sun more glad impress'd his beams
Than in fair evening cloud, or humid bow,

When God hath shower'd the earth: so lovely seem'd
That landskip.

From *Paradise Lost*, IV.

1674

༄

John Evelyn
Of the Hasel

1. *Nux Sylvestris*, or *Corylus*, the *Hasel*, is best rais'd from the *Nuts*, (also by *Suckers* and *Layers*) which you shall sow like *Mast*, in a pretty deep *furrow* toward the end of *February*, or treat them as you are instructed in the *Wal-nut*; Light ground may immediately be sown and *harrow'd* in very accurately; but in case the mould be *clay*, plow it earlier, and let it be sufficiently mellow'd with the *Frosts*; and then the third year, cut your *Trees* near to the ground with a sharp *bill*, the *Moon* decreasing.

2. But if you would make a *Grove* for Pleasure, *Plant* them in *Fasses*, at a *yard* distance, and *cut* them within half a foot of the earth, dressing them for three, or four *Springs* and *Autumns*, by only loosning the *Mould* a little about their roots. Others there are, who set the *Nuts* by hand at one foot distance, to be *transplanted* the third year at a yard asunder: But this work is not to be taken in hand so soon as the *Nuts* fall, till *Winter* be well advanc'd; because they are exceedingly obnoxious to the *Frosts*; nor will they sprout till the *Spring*; besides, *Vermine* are great devourers of them: Preserve them therefore *moist*, not *mouldy*; by laying them in their own *dry* leaves, or in *Sand*, till *January*.

3. From whence they thrive very well, the *shoots* being of the scantlings of small *wands*, and *switches*, or somewhat bigger, and such as have drawn divers *hairy* twiggs, which are by no means to be disbranch'd, no more than their *Roots*, unless by a very sparing and discreet hand. Thus, your *Coryletum*, or *Copp'ce* of *Hasels* being Planted about *Autumn*, may (as some practise it) be cut within three, or four inches of the ground the *Spring* following, which the new *Cyon* will suddenly repair, in clusters,

and tufts of fair *poles* of twenty, and sometimes thirty foot long: But I rather should spare them till two, or three years after, when they shall have taken strong hold, and may be cut close to the very Earth; the improsperous, and feeble ones especially. Thus are likewise *Filberts* to be treated, both of them improv'd much by transplanting, but chiefly by *Graffing*, and it would be try'd with *Filberts*, and even with *Almonds* themselves, for more elegant Experiments.

4. For the *Place*, they above all affect *cold, barren, dry*, and *Sandy* grounds; also *Mountains*, and even *Rockie* Soils produce them; but more plentifully, if somewhat moist, dankish, and mossie, as in the fresher *bottoms*, and sides of *Hills, Hoults*, and in *Hedg-rows*. Such as are maintain'd for *Copp'ces*, may after Twelve years be *fell'd* the first time; the next, at seven or eight, *etc.* for by this period, their *Roots* will be compleatly vigorous. You may *Plant* them from *October* to *January*, provided you keep them carefully *Weeded*, till they have taken fast hold; and there is not among all our store, a more profitable wood for *Copp'ces*, and therefore good *Husbands* should store them with it.

5. The use of the *Hasel* is for *Poles, Spars, Hoops, Forks, Angling-rods, Faggots, Cudgels, Coals*, and *Springes* to catch *birds*; and it makes one of the best *Coals*, once us'd for *Gun-powder*, being very fine and Light, till they found *Alder* to be more fit: There is no Wood which purifies *Wine* sooner, than the *Chips* of *Hasel*: Also for *With's* and *Bands*, upon which, I remember *Pliny* thinks it a pretty *Speculation*, that a Wood should be stronger to bind withal, being *bruis'd* and *Divided*, than when *whole* and *entire*; The *Coals* are us'd by *Painters*, to draw with like those of *Sallow*: lastly, for Riding *Switches*, and *Divinatory Rods* for the detecting, and finding-out of *Minerals*; at least, if that *Tradition* be no imposture. But the most signal Honour it was ever employ'd in, and which might deservedly exalt this humble, and common *Plant* above all the *Trees* of the *Wood*, is that of *Hurdles*; not for that it is generally us'd for the Folding of our Innocent *Sheep*, an Emblem of the *Church*; but for making the *Walls* of one of the first *Christian Oratories* in the World; and particularly in this *Island*, that venerable, and Sacred Fabrick at Glastonbury, founded by *S. Joseph* of *Arimathea*, which is storied to have been first compos'd but of a few small *Hasel-Rods* interwoven about certain *Stakes* driven into the ground; and Walls of this kind, instead of *Laths* and *Punchions*, super-

induc'd with a course *Mortar* made of *loam* and *straw*, does to this day, inclose divers humble *Cottages, Sheads* and *Out-houses* in the Countrey; and 'tis strong, and lasting for such purposes, *whole*, or *cleft*, and I have seen ample enclosures of *Courts*, and *Gardens* so secur'd.

6. There is a compendious expedient for the thickning of *Copp'ces* which are too *transparent*, by laying of a *Sampler* or *Pole* of an *Hasel, Ash, Poplar, etc.* of twenty, or thirty foot in length (the head a little lopp'd) into the ground, giving it a *Chop* near the foot, to make it succumb; *this* fastned to the earth with a *hook* or two, and cover'd with some fresh *mould* at a competent depth (as *Gardeners* lay their *Carnations*) will produce a world of *Suckers*, thicken, and furnish a *Copp'ce* speedily. But I am now come to the *Water-side*; let us next consider the *Aquatic*.

From Sylva, or a Discourse of Forest-trees and the Propagation of Timber
in His Majesties Dominions.

1679

King Charles II

[The King tells Samuel Pepys how he hid in an Oak after the Battle of Worcester]

We went on our way to one of Penderell's brothers, (his house being not far from White Ladys) who had been guide to my Lord Wilmot, and we believed might, by that time, be come back again; for my Lord Wilmot intended to go to London upon his own horse. When I came to this house, I inquired where my Lord Wilmot was; it being now towards morning, and having travelled these two nights on foot, Penderell's brother told me, that he had conducted him to a very honest gentleman's house, one Mr. Pitchcroft, not far from Woolverhampton, a Roman Catholic. I asked him, what news? He told me, that there was one Major Careless in the house that was that country-man; whom I knowing, he having been a major in our army, and made his escape thither, a Roman Catholic also, I sent for him into the room where I was, and consulting with him what we should do the next day. He told me, that it would be very dangerous for me either to stay in that house, or to go into the wood, there being a great wood hard by Boscobel; that he knew but one way how to pass the next day, and that was, to get up into a great oak, in a pretty plain place, where we might see round about us; for the enemy would certainly search at the wood for people that had made their escape. Of which proposition of his I approving, we (that is to say, Careless and I) went, and carried up with us some victuals for the whole day, viz. bread, cheese, small bear, and nothing else, and got up into a great oak, that had been lopt some three or four years before, and being grown out again, very bushy and thick, could not be seen through, and here we staid all the day. I having, in the mean time, sent Penderell's brother to Mr. Pitchcroft's, to know whether my Lord Wilmot was there or no; and had word brought me by him, at night, that my Lord was there: that there was a very secure hiding-hole in Mr. Pitchcroft's house, and that he desired me to come thither to him.

Memorandum, That while we were in this tree we see soldiers going up and down, in the thicket of the wood, searching for persons escaped, we seeing them, now and then, peeping out of the wood.

From An Account of his Majesty's escape from Worcester,
dictated to Mr. Pepys by the King himself.

1680

ℱ๑

Anonymous

[Zaccheus]

Zaccheus he
Did climb the Tree
His Lord to see.

From *The New England Primer*.

ca. 1690

Anonymous
["Beware"]

Beware of an oak,
It draws the stroke.
Avoid an ash,
It courts the flash.
Creep under the thorn,
It will save you from harm.

———————

Folk Saw.

ca. 1700

Anonymous
[Oak and Ash]

Oak before Ash,
Spring comes with a splash;
Ash before oak,
It comes with a soak.

———————

Folk saw.

ca. 1700

Anonymous
[The twelve days of Christmas]

The twelfth day of Christmas,
My true love sent to me
Twelve lords a-leaping,
Eleven ladies dancing,
Ten pipers piping,
Nine drummers drumming,
Eight maids a-milking,
Seven swans a-swimming,
Six geese a-laying,
Five gold rings,
Four colly birds,
Three French hens,
Two turtle doves, and
A partridge in a pear tree.

---

ca. 18th century

Alexander Pope
["Order in variety"]

The groves of Eden, vanish'd now so long,
Live in description, and look green in song:
These, were my breast inspired with equal flame,
Like them in beauty, should be like in fame.
Here hills and vales, the woodland and the plain,
Here earth and water seem to strive again;
Not chaos-like together crush'd and bruised,
But, as the world harmoniously confused:
Where order in variety we see,

71

And where, though all things differ, all agree.
Here waving groves a chequer'd scene display,
And part admit, and part exclude the day;
As some coy nymph her lover's warm address
Not quite indulges, nor can quite repress.
There, interspersed in lawns and opening glades,
Thin trees arise that shun each other's shades.
Here in full light the russet plains extend:
There, wrapt in clouds the bluish hills ascend.
Even the wild heath displays her purple dyes,
And 'midst the desert, fruitful fields arise,
That crown'd with tufted trees and springing corn,
Like verdant isles the sable waste adorn.
Let India boast her plants, nor envy we
The weeping amber, or the balmy tree,
While by our oaks the precious loads are borne,
And realms commanded which those trees adorn.
Not proud Olympus yields a nobler sight,
Though gods assembled grace his towering height,
Than what more humble mountains offer here,
Where, in their blessings, all those gods appear.

From "Windsor Forest."

1713

~

Daniel Defoe

[Crusoe and Friday make a Boat]

... I found a strong inclination to attempting an escape, as above, founded on the supposition gathered from the former discourse, namely, that there were seventeen bearded men there; and therefore, without any more delay, I went to work with Friday, to find out a great tree proper to fell, and make a large periagua, or canoe, for the voyage. After searching some time, Friday at last pitched upon a tree, for I found he knew much better than I what kind of wood was fittest for it; nor can I tell, to this day, what wood to call the tree we cut down, except that it was very like the tree we call fustic, or between that and the Nicaragua wood, for it was much of the same colour and smell. Friday was for burning the hollow or cavity of this tree out, to make it into a boat; but I showed him how rather to cut it out with tools, which after I showed him how to use he did it very handily, and in about a month's hard labour we finished it and made it very handsome, especially when with our axes, which I showed him how to handle, we cut and hewed the outside into the true shape of a boat. After this, however, it cost us near a fortnight's time to get her along, as it were, inch by inch, upon great rollers, into the water; but when she was in, she would have carried twenty men with ease.

It amazed me to see with what dexterity and how swift my man Friday would manage her, turn her, and paddle her along. So I asked him if he would, and if we might venture over in her. "Yes," he said, "me venture over in her very well, though great blow wind." However, I had a further design that he knew nothing of, and that was to make a mast and a sail, and to fit her with an anchor and a cable. As to the mast, that was easy enough to get, so I pitched upon a straight young cedar tree, which I found near the place, and which there was plenty of in the island; and I set Friday to work to cut it down, and gave him directions how to shape and order it. But as to the sail, that was my particular care.

From *Robinson Crusoe*, XVIII.

1719

William Byrd

["The Pines in this part of the country"]

The Pines in this part of the country are of a different Species from those that grow in Virginia: their bearded Leaves are much longer and their Cones much larger. Each Cell contains a Seed of the Size and Figure of a black-ey'd Pea, which, Shedding in November, is a very good Mast for Hogs, and fattens them in a Short time. The smallest of these Pines are full of Cones, which are 8 or 9 Inches long, and each affords commonly 60 or 70 Seeds. This Kind of Mast has the Advantage of all other, by being more constant, and less liable to be nippt by the Frost, or eaten by the Caterpillars. The Trees also abound more with Turpentine, and consequently yield more Tarr, than either the Yellow or the White Pine; and for the same reason make more durable Timber for building. The Inhabitants hereabouts pick up Knots of Lightwood in abundance, which they burn into tar, and then carry it to Norfolk or Nansemond for a Market. The Tar made in this method is the less Valuable, because it is said to burn the Cordage, tho' it is full as good for all other uses, as that made in Sweden and Muscovy.

From *The History of the Dividing Line* [between Virginia and North Carolina].

1728

Gilbert White

[Memorable Trees]

In the court of Norton farm house, a manor farm to the north-west of the village, on the white malm, stood within these twenty years a broad-leaved elm, or wych hazel, *ulmus folio latissimo scabro* of Ray, which, although it had lost a considerable leading bough in the great storm in the year 1703, equal to a moderate tree, yet, when felled, contained eight loads of timber; and, being too bulky for a carriage, was sawn off at seven feet above the butt, where it measured near eight feet in the diameter. This elm I mention to show to what a bulk *planted elms* may attain; as this tree must certainly have been such from its situation.

In the centre of the village, and near the church, is a square piece of ground surrounded by houses and vulgarly called The Plestor. In the midst of this spot stood, in old times, a vast oak, with a short squat body, and huge horizontal arms extending almost to the extremity of the area. This venerable tree, surrounded with stone steps, and seats above them, was the de-

Notting Hill in 1750.

From *Old and New London,* ca. 1875

View From "Moll King's House," Hampstead, in 1760.

From *Old and New London,* ca. 1875

light of old and young, and a place of much resort in summer evenings; where the former sat in grave debate, while the latter frolicked and danced before them. Long might it have stood, had not the amazing tempest in 1703 overturned it at once, to the infinite regret of the inhabitants, and the vicar, who bestowed several pounds in setting it in its place again: but all his care could not avail; the tree sprouted for a time, then withered and died....

On the Blackmoor estate there is a small wood called Losel's, of a few acres, that was lately furnished with a set of oaks of a peculiar growth and great value; they were tall and taper like firs, but standing near together had very small heads, only a little brush without any large limbs. About twenty years ago the bridge at the Toy, near Hampton Court, being much decayed, some trees were wanted for the repairs that were fifty feet long without bough, and would measure twelve inches diameter at the little end. Twenty such trees did a purveyor find in this little wood, with this advantage, that many of them answered the description at sixty feet. These trees were sold for twenty pounds apiece.

In the centre of this grove there stood an oak, which, though shapely and tall on the whole, bulged out into a large excrescence about the middle of the stem. On this a pair of ravens had fixed their residence for such a series of years, that the oak was distinguished by the title of The Raven-tree. Many were the attempts of the neighbouring youths to get at this eyry: the difficulty whetted their inclinations, and each was ambitious of surmounting the arduous task. But, when they arrived at the swelling, it jutted out so in their way, and was so far beyond their grasp, that the most daring lads were awed, and acknowledged the undertaking to be too hazardous. So the ravens built on, nest upon nest, in perfect security, till the fatal day arrived in which the wood was to be levelled. It was in the month of February, when these birds usually sit. The saw was applied to the butt, the wedges were inserted into the opening, the woods echoed to the heavy blow of the beetle or malle or mallet, the tree nodded to its fall; but still the dam sat on. At last, when it gave way, the bird was flung from her nest; and, though her parental affection deserved a better fate, was whipped down by the twigs, which brought her dead to the ground.

From *The Natural History of Selborne*, Letter 2.

1767

William Cowper

The Shrubbery
Written in a Time of Affliction

Oh, happy shades – to me unblest!
　　Friendly to peace, but not to me!
How ill the scene that offers rest,
　　And heart that cannot rest, agree!

This glassy stream, that spreading pine,
　　Those alders quiv'ring to the breeze,
Might soothe a soul less hurt than mine,
　　And please, if any thing could please.

But fix'd unalterable care
　　Foregoes not what she feels within,
Shows the same sadness ev'ry where,
　　And slights the season and the scene.

For all that pleas'd in wood or lawn,
　　While peace possess'd these silent bow'rs,
Her animating smile withdrawn,
　　Has lost its beauties and its pow'rs.

The saint or moralist should tread
　　This moss-grown alley, musing, slow;
They seek, like me, the secret shade,
　　But not, like me, to nourish woe!

Me fruitful scenes and prospects waste
　　Alike admonish not to roam;
These tell me of enjoyments past,
　　And those of sorrows yet to come.

---

ca. 1781

William Gilpin, [view of Tintern Abbey].
From Observations on the River Wye.

1782

Alexander Cozens, [trees beside a stream]. From A New Method of Assisting
the Invention in Drawing Original Compositions of Landscape.

ca. 1785

George Crabbe
[The aged villager's complaint]

Like leaves in spring, the young are blown away,
Without the sorrows of a slow decay;
I, like yon withered leaf, remain behind,
Nipped by the frost and shivering in the wind;
There it abides till younger buds come on,
As I, now all my fellow-swains are gone;
Then, from the rising generation thrust,
It falls, like me, unnoticed to the dust.

From *The Village*, I.

1783

William Cowper
["The woodland scene"]

There from the sun-burnt hay-field, homeward creeps
The loaded wain; while, lighten'd of its charge,
The wain that meets it passes swiftly by;
The boorish driver leaning o'er his team
Vocif'rous, and impatient of delay.
Nor less attractive is the woodland scene,
Diversified with trees of ev'ry growth,
Alike, yet various. Here the gray smooth trunks
Of ash, or lime, or beech, distinctly shine,
Within the twilight of their distant shades;
There, lost behind a rising ground, the wood
Seems sunk, and shorten'd to its topmost boughs.
No tree in all the grove but has its charms,

Though each its hue peculiar; paler some,
And of a wannish gray; the willow such,
And poplar, that with silver lines his leaf,
And ash far-stretching his umbrageous arm;
Of deeper green the elm; and deeper still,
Lord of the woods, the long-surviving oak.
Some glossy-leav'd, and shining in the sun,
The maple, and the beech of oily nuts
Prolific, and the lime at dewy eve
Diffusing odours: nor unnoted pass
The sycamore, capricious in attire,
Now green, now tawny, and, ere autumn yet
Have chang'd the woods, in scarlet honours bright.
O'er these, but far beyond (a spacious map
Of hill and valley interpos'd between),
The Ouse, dividing the well-water'd land,
Now glitters in the sun, and now retires,
As bashful, yet impatient to be seen.

From *The Task*, I.

1785

William Cowper
The Poplar Field

The poplars are felled; farewell to the shade,
And the whispering sound of the cool colonnade!
The winds play no longer and sing in the leaves,
Nor Ouse on his bosom their image receives.

Twelve years have elapsed since I first took a view
Of my favourite field, and the bank where they grew;
And now in the grass behold they are laid,
And the tree is my seat that once lent me a shade!

The blackbird has fled to another retreat,
Where the hazels afford him a screen from the heat,
And the scene where his melody charmed me before,
Resounds with his sweet-flowing ditty no more.

My fugitive years are all hasting away,
And I must ere long lie as lowly as they,
With a turf on my breast, and a stone at my head,
Ere another such grove shall arise in its stead.

'Tis a sight to engage me, if anything can,
To muse on the perishing pleasures of man;
Though his life be a dream, his enjoyments, I see,
Have a being less durable even than he.

ca. 1792

William Blake, title page from Songs of Innocence.

1789

The Botanical Gardens, Chelsea, 1790.
From *Old and New London,* ca. 1875.

Robert Burns
Their Groves o' Sweet Myrtle

Their groves o' sweet myrtle let foreign lands reckon,
    Where bright-beaming summers exalt the perfume;
Far dearer to me yon lone glen o' green breckan,
    Wi' the burn stealing under the lang yellow broom.

Far dearer to me are yon humble broom bowers,
    Where the blue-bell and gowan lurk lowly unseen:
For there, lightly tripping amang the wild flowers,
    A-listening the linnet, aft wanders my Jean.

Tho' rich is the breeze in their gay sunny valleys,
    And cauld Caledonia's blast on the wave;
Their sweet-scented woodlands that skirt the proud palace,
    What are they? The haunt of the tyrant and slave!

The slave's spicy forests, and gold-bubbling fountains,
    The brave Caledonian views wi' disdain;
He wanders as free as the winds of his mountains,
    Save Love's willing fetters, the chains o' his Jean.

—————

1795

Mary Wollstonecraft
["The pine and fir woods"]

I have often mentioned the grandeur, but I feel myself unequal to the task of conveying an idea of the beauty and elegance of the scene when the spiral tops of the pines are loaded with ripening seed, and the sun gives a glow to their light green tinge, which is changing into purple, one tree more or less advanced, contrasting with another. The profusion with which nature has decked them, with pendant honours, prevents all surprise at seeing, in every crevice, some sapling struggling for existence. Vast masses of stone are thus encircled; and roots, torn up by the storms, become a shelter for a young generation. The pine and fir woods, left entirely to nature, display an endless variety; and the paths in the wood are not entangled with fallen leaves, which are only interesting whilst they are fluttering between life and death. The grey cobweb-like appearance of the aged pines is a much finer image of decay; the fibres whitening as they lose their moisture, imprisoned life seems to be stealing away. I cannot tell why – but death, under every form, appears to me like something getting free – to expand in I know not what element; nay I feel that this conscious being must be as unfettered, have the wings of thought, before it can be happy.

From Letter XV, *Letters Written During a Short Residence in Sweden, Norway, and Denmark.*

1796

❧

William Wordsworth
[Dancing leaves]

A whirl-blast from behind the hill
Rushed o'er the wood with startling sound;
Then – all at once the air was still,
And showers of hailstones pattered round.
Where leafless oaks towered high above,
I sat within an undergrove
Of tallest hollies, tall and green;
A fairer bower was never seen.
From year to year the spacious floor
With withered leaves is covered o'er,
And all the year the bower is green.

But see! where'er the hailstones drop
The withered leaves all skip and hop;
There's not a breeze – no breath of air –
Yet here, and there, and every where
Along the floor, beneath the shade
By those embowering hollies made,
The leaves in myriads jump and spring,
As if with pipes and music rare
Some Robin Good-fellow were there,
And all those leaves, in festive glee,
Were dancing to the minstrelsy.

———

1798

William Wordsworth

["This poor Thorn"]

"There is a Thorn – it looks so old,
In truth, you'd find it hard to say
How it could ever have been young,
It looks so old and grey,
Not higher than a two years' child
It stands erect, this aged Thorn;
No leaves it has, no prickly points,
It is a mass of knotted joints,
A wretched thing forlorn,
It stands erect, and like a stone
With lichens is it overgrown.

"Like rock or stone, it is o'ergrown,
With lichens to the very top,
And hung with heavy tufts of moss,
A melancholy crop:
Up from the earth these mosses creep,
And this poor Thorn they clasp it round
So close, you'd say that they are bent
With plain and manifest intent
To drag it to the ground;
And all have joined in one endeavour
To bury this poor Thorn for ever."

From "The Thorn".

1798

Robert Southey
The Holly Tree

O Reader! hast thou ever stood to see
    The Holly Tree?
The eye that contemplates it well perceives
    Its glossy leaves
Order'd by an intelligence so wise,
As might confound the Atheist's sophistries.

Below, a circling fence, its leaves are seen
    Wrinkled and keen;
No grazing cattle through their prickly round
    Can reach to wound;
But as they grow where nothing is to fear,
Smooth and unarm'd the pointless leaves appear.

I love to view these things with curious eyes,
    And moralize;
And in this wisdom of the Holly Tree
    Can emblems see
Wherewith perchance to make a pleasant rhyme,
One which may profit in the after time.

Thus, though abroad perchance I might appear
    Harsh and austere,
To those who on my leisure would intrude
    Reserved and rude,
Gentle at home amid my friends I'd be
Like the high leaves upon the Holly Tree.

And should my youth, as youth is apt I know,
    Some harshness show,
All vain asperities I day by day
    Would wear away,
Till the smooth temper of my age should be
Like the high leaves upon the Holly Tree.

And as when all the summer trees are seen
    So bright and green,
The Holly leaves a sober hue display
    Less bright then they,
But when the bare and wintry woods we see,
    What then so cheerful as the Holly Tree?

So serious should my youth appear among
    The thoughtless throng,
So would I seem amid the young and gay
    More grave than they,
That in my age as cheerful I might be
As the green winter of the Holly Tree.

1798

₫₫

William Wordsworth
Nutting

– – – – – – – – – – – – It seems a day
(I speak of one from many singled out)
One of those heavenly days that cannot die;
When, in the eagerness of boyish hope,
I left our cottage-threshold, sallying forth
With a huge wallet o'er my shoulders slung,
A nutting-crook in hand; and turned my steps
Tow'rd some far-distant wood, a Figure quaint,

Tricked out in proud disguise of cast-off weeds
Which for that service had been husbanded,
By exhortation of my frugal Dame –
Motley accoutrement, of power to smile
At thorns, and brakes, and brambles – and in truth
More ragged than need was! O'er pathless rocks,
Through beds of matted fern, and tangled thickets,
Forcing my way, I came to one dear nook
Unvisited, where not a broken bough
Drooped with its withered leaves, ungracious sign
Of devastation; but the hazels rose
Tall and erect, with tempting clusters hung,
A virgin scene! – A little while I stood,
Breathing with such suppression of the heart
As joy delights in; and with wise restraint
Voluptuous, fearless of a rival, eyed
The banquet; – or beneath the trees I sate
Among the flowers, and with the flowers I played;
A temper known to those who, after long
And weary expectation, have been blest
With sudden happiness beyond all hope.
Perhaps it was a bower beneath whose leaves
The violets of five seasons re-appear
And fade, unseen by any human eye;
Where fairy water-breaks do murmur on
For ever; and I saw the sparkling foam,
And – with my cheek on one of those green stones
That, fleeced with moss, under the shady trees,
Lay round me, scattered like a flock of sheep –
I heard the murmur and the murmuring sound,
In that sweet mood when pleasure loves to pay
Tribute to ease; and, of its joy secure,
The heart luxuriates with indifferent things,
Wasting its kindliness on stocks and stones,
And on the vacant air. Then up I rose,
And dragged to earth both branch and bough, with crash

And merciless ravage; and the shady nook
Of hazels, and the green and mossy bower,
Deformed and sullied, patiently gave up
Their quiet being: and unless I now
Confound my present feelings with the past,
Ere from the mutilated bower I turned
Exulting, rich beyond the wealth of kings,
I felt a sense of pain when I beheld
The silent trees, and saw the intruding sky. –
Then, dearest Maiden, move along these shades
In gentleness of heart; with gentle hand
Touch – for there is a spirit in the woods.

1798

∿

William Wordsworth

[Nature's lore]

One impulse from a vernal wood
May teach you more of man,
Of moral evil and of good,
Than all the sages can.

Sweet is the lore which Nature brings;
Our meddling intellect
Mis-shapes the beauteous forms of things: –
We murder to dissect.

Enough of Science and of Art;
Close up those barren leaves;
Come forth, and bring with you a heart
That watches and receives.

From "The Tables Turned".

1798

John Constable, "Study of Ash and Other Trees."

By courtesy of the Board of Trustees of the Victoria & Albert Museum.

1800-5

§

Samuel Taylor Coleridge
This Lime-Tree Bower My Prison

Addressed to Charles Lamb, of the India House, London

Well, they are gone, and here must I remain,
This lime-tree bower my prison! I have lost
Beauties and feelings, such as would have been
Most sweet to my remembrance even when age
Had dimmed mine eyes to blindness! They, meanwhile,
Friends, whom I never more may meet again,
On springy heath, along the hill-top edge,
Wander in gladness, and wind down, perchance,
To that still roaring dell, of which I told;
The roaring dell, o'erwooded, narrow, deep,
And only speckled by the mid-day sun;
Where its slim trunk the ash from rock to rock
Flings arching like a bridge; – that branchless ash,
Unsunned and damp, whose few poor yellow leaves
Ne'er tremble in the gale, yet tremble still,
Fanned by the waterfall! and there my friends
Behold the dark green file of long lank weeds,
That all at once (a most fantastic sight!)
Still nod and drip beneath the dripping edge
Of the blue clay-stone.
                 Now, my friends emerge
Beneath the wide wide Heaven – and view again
The many-steepled tract magnificent
Of hilly fields and meadows, and the sea,
With some fair bark, perhaps, whose sails light up
The slip of smooth clear blue betwixt two Isles
Of purple shadow! Yes! they wander on
In gladness all; but thou, methinks, most glad,
My gentle-hearted Charles! for thou hast pined

And hungered after Nature, many a year,
In the great City pent, winning thy way
With sad yet patient soul, through evil and pain
And strange calamity! Ah! slowly sink
Behind the western ridge, thou glorious Sun!
Shine in the slant beams of the sinking orb,
Ye purple heath-flowers! richlier burn, ye clouds!
Live in the yellow light, ye distant groves!
And kindle, thou blue Ocean! So my friend
Struck with deep joy may stand, as I have stood,
Silent with swimming sense; yea, gazing round
On the wide landscape, gaze till all doth seem
Less gross than bodily; and of such hues
As veil the Almighty Spirit, when yet he makes
Spirits perceive his presence.
                                    A delight
Comes sudden on my heart, and I am glad
As I myself were there! Nor in this bower,
This little lime-tree bower, have I not marked
Much that has soothed me. Pale beneath the blaze
Hung the transparent foliage; and I watched
Some broad and sunny leaf, and loved to see
The shadow of the leaf and stem above
Dappling its sunshine! And that walnut-tree
Was richly tinged, and a deep radiance lay
Full on the ancient ivy, which usurps
Those fronting elms, and now, with blackest mass
Makes their dark branches gleam a lighter hue
Through the late twilight: and though now the bat
Wheels silent by, and not a swallow twitters,
Yet still the solitary humblebee
Sings in the bean-flower! Henceforth I shall know
That Nature ne'er deserts the wise and pure;
No plot so narrow, be but Nature there,
No waste so vacant, but may well employ

J. M. W. Turner, "Windsor from the Forest." Engraved by J. Greig.

1804

Each faculty of sense, and keep the heart
Awake to Love and Beauty! and sometimes
'Tis well to be bereft of promised good,
That we may lift the soul, and contemplate
With lively joys the joys we cannot share.
My gentle-hearted Charles! when the last rook
Beat its straight path along the dusky air
Homewards, I blessed it! deeming its black wing
(Now a dim speck, now vanishing in light)
Had crossed the mighty Orb's dilated glory,
While thou stood'st gazing; or, when all was still,
Flew creeking o'er thy head, and had a charm
For thee, my gentle-hearted Charles, to whom
No sound is dissonant which tells of Life.

1800

Jane Austen

[Improvements]

After a short interruption, Mr. Rushworth began again. "Smith's place is the admiration of all the country; and it was a mere nothing before Repton took it in hand. I think I shall have Repton."

....

Edmund was glad to put an end to his speech by a proposal of wine. Mr. Rushworth, however, though not usually a great talker, had still more to say on the subject next his heart. "Smith has not much above a hundred acres altogether in his grounds, which is little enough, and makes it more surprising that the place can have been so improved. Now, at Sotherton, we have a good seven hundred, without reckoning the water meadows; so that I think, if so much could be done at Compton, we need not despair. There have been two or three fine old trees cut down that grew too near the house, and it opens the prospect amazingly,

"The Cross in the Mountains" (Tetschen Altarpiece),
by Caspar David Friedrich.

Reproduced with the permission of Sächsische
Landesbibliothek, Dresden.

1807-8

which makes me think that Repton, or any body of that sort, would certainly have the avenue at Sotherton down; the avenue that leads from the west front to the top of the hill you know," turning to Miss Bertram particularly as he spoke. But Miss Bertram thought it most becoming to reply:

"The avenue! Oh! I do not recollect it. I really know very little of Sotherton."

Fanny, who was sitting on the other side of Edmund, exactly opposite Miss Crawford, and who had been attentively listening, now looked at him, and said in a low voice,

"Cut down an avenue! What a pity! Does not it make you think of Cowper? 'Ye fallen avenues, once more I mourn your fate unmerited.'"

He smiled as he answered, "I am afraid the avenue stands a bad chance, Fanny."

"I should like to see Sotherton before it is cut down, to see the place as it is now, in its old state; but I do not suppose I shall."

From *Mansfield Park*, VI.

1814

❆

John Leyden
Sonnet to the Yew-Tree

When Fortune smiled, and Nature's charms were new,
   I loved to see the oak majestic tower, –
   I loved to see the apple's painted flower,
Bedropt with penciled tints of rosy hue:
Now more I love thee, melancholy Yew,
Whose still green leaves in solemn silence wave
Above the peasant's rude unhonour'd grave,
Which oft thou moisten'st with the morning dew.
To thee the sad – to thee the weary fly;

They rest in peace beneath thy sacred gloom,
Thou sole companion of the lonely tomb;
No leaves but thine in pity o'er them sigh:
Lo! now to Fancy's gaze thou seem'st to spread
Thy shadowy boughs, to shroud me with the dead.

Blackwood's Edinburgh Magazine, I.

1817

‫ؖ‬

John Keats
[A hymn to Pan]

O thou, whose mighty palace roof doth hang
From jagged trunks, and overshadoweth
Eternal whispers, glooms, the birth, life, death,
Of unseen flowers in heavy peacefulness;
Who lov'st to see the hamadryads dress
Their ruffled locks where meeting hazels darken;
And through whole solemn hours dost sit, and hearken
The dreary melody of bedded reeds –
In desolate places, where dank moisture breeds
The pipy hemlock to strange overgrowth;
Bethinking thee, how melancholy loth
Thou wast to lose fair Syrinx – do thou now,
By thy love's milky brow!
By all the trembling mazes that she ran,
Hear us, great Pan!

From *Endymion*, I.

1818

John Constable, "Study of Ash Trees."

By courtesy of the Board of Trustees of the Victoria & Albert Museum.

1817-19

ℱ

Percy Bysshe Shelley
Ode to the West Wind

1

O wild West Wind, thou breath of Autumn's being,
Thou, from whose unseen presence the leaves dead
Are driven, like ghosts from an enchanter fleeing,

Yellow, and black, and pale, and hectic red,
Pestilence-stricken multitudes: O thou,
Who chariotest to their dark wintry bed

The wingèd seeds, where they lie cold and low,
Each like a corpse within its grave, until
Thine azure sister of the Spring shall blow

Her clarion o'er the dreaming earth, and fill
(Driving sweet buds like flocks to feed in air)
With living hues and odours plain and hill:

Wild Spirit, which art moving everywhere;
Destroyer and preserver; hear, oh, hear!

2

Thou on whose stream, mid the steep sky's commotion,
Loose clouds like earth's decaying leaves are shed,
Shook from the tangled boughs of Heaven and Ocean,

Angels of rain and lightning: there are spread
On the blue surface of thine aëry surge,
Like the bright hair uplifted from the head

Of some fierce Maenad, even from the dim verge
Of the horizon to the zenith's height,
The locks of the approaching storm. Thou dirge

Of the dying year, to which this closing night
Will be the dome of a vast sepulchre,
Vaulted with all thy congregated might

Of vapours, from whose solid atmosphere
Black rain, and fire, and hail will burst: oh, hear!

3

Thou who didst waken from his summer dreams
The blue Mediterranean, where he lay,
Lulled by the coil of his crystàlline streams,

Beside a pumice isle in Baiae's bay,
And saw in sleep old palaces and towers
Quivering within the wave's intenser day,

All overgrown with azure moss and flowers
So sweet, the sense faints picturing them! Thou
For whose path the Atlantic's level powers

Cleave themselves into chasms, while far below
The sea-blooms and the oozy woods which wear
The sapless foliage of the ocean, know

Thy voice, and suddenly grow gray with fear,
And tremble and despoil themselves: oh, hear!

4

If I were a dead leaf thou mightest bear;
If I were a swift cloud to fly with thee;
A wave to pant beneath thy power, and share

The impulse of thy strength, only less free
Than thou, O uncontrollable! If even
I were as in my boyhood, and could be

The comrade of thy wanderings over Heaven,
As then, when to outstrip thy skiey speed
Scarce seemed a vision; I would ne'er have striven

As thus with thee in prayer in my sore need.
Oh, lift me as a wave, a leaf, a cloud!
I fall upon the thorns of life! I bleed!

A heavy weight of hours has chained and bowed
One too like thee: tameless, and swift, and proud.

5

Make me thy lyre, even as the forest is:
What if my leaves are falling like its own!
The tumult of thy mighty harmonies

Will take from both a deep autumnal tone,
Sweet though in sadness. Be thou, Spirit fierce,
My spirit! Be thou me, impetuous one!

Drive my dead thoughts over the universe
Like withered leaves to quicken a new birth!
And, by the incantation of this verse,

Scatter, as from an unextinguished hearth
Ashes and sparks, my words among mankind!
Be through my lips to unawakened earth

The trumpet of a prophecy! O Wind,
If Winter comes, can Spring be far behind?

1819

J. M. W. Turner, "Lake of Nemi." Engraved by Samuel Middiman
and John Pye.

1819

Johann Wyss

["This glorious palace of the woods"]

"We at length approached my pretty wood. Numbers of birds fluttered and sang among the high branches, but I did not encourage the boys in their wish to try to shoot any of the happy little creatures. We were lost in admiration of the trees in this grove, and I cannot describe to you how wonderful they are, nor can you form the least idea of their enormous size without seeing them yourself. What we had been calling a wood proved to be a group of about a dozen trees only, and, what was strange, the roots sustained the massive trunks exalted in the air, forming strong arches, and props and stays all around each individual stem, which was firmly rooted in the center.

"I gave Jack some twine, and scrambling up one of the curious open-air roots, he succeeded in measuring round the trunk itself, and made it out to be about eighteen yards. I saw no sort of fruit, but the foliage is thick and abundant, throwing delicious shade on the ground beneath, which is carpeted with soft green herbage, and entirely free from thorns, briers, or bushes of any kind. It is the most charming resting place that ever was seen, and I and the boys enjoyed our midday meal immensely in this glorious palace of the woods, so grateful to our senses after the glare and heat of our journey thither. The dogs joined us after a while. They had lingered behind on the seashore, and I was surprised to see them lie down and go comfortably to sleep without begging for food, as they do usually when we eat.

"The longer we remained in this enchanting place the more did it charm my fancy; and if we could but manage to live in some sort of dwelling up among the branches of those grand, noble trees, I should feel perfectly safe and happy. It seemed to me absurd to suppose we should ever find another place half so lovely, so I determined to search no farther, but return to the beach and see if anything from the wreck had been cast up by the waves, which we could carry away with us."

. . . .

"What sort of a tree do you suppose this to be, father?" inquired Ernest, seeing me examining that under which we were encamping. "Is not the leaf something like the walnut?"

"There is a resemblance, but in my opinion these gigantic trees must be mangroves, or wild figs. I have heard their enormous height described, and also the peculiarity of the arching roots supporting the main trunk raised above the soil."

From *The Swiss Family Robinson*, III.

ca. 1820

John Keats

[*"Green-rob'd senators of mighty woods"*]

"Saturn, sleep on: – O thoughtless, why did I
Thus violate thy slumbrous solitude?
Why should I ope thy melancholy eyes?
Saturn, sleep on! while at thy feet I weep."
   As when, upon a tranced summer-night,
Those green-rob'd senators of mighty woods,
Tall oaks, branch-charmed by the earnest stars,
Dream, and so dream all night without a stir,
Save from one gradual solitary gust
Which comes upon the silence, and dies off,
As if the ebbing air had but one wave;
So came these words and went; the while in tears
She touch'd her fair large forehead to the ground....

From *Hyperion*, I.

1820

John Constable, "Fir Trees at Hampstead."

By courtesy of the Victoria & Albert Museum.

1820

William Wordsworth
["Triumphant Memory"]

Whence that low voice? – A whisper from the heart,
That told of days long past, when here I roved
With friends and kindred tenderly beloved;
Some who had early mandates to depart,
Yet are allowed to steal my path athwart
By Duddon's side; once more do we unite,
Once more beneath the kind Earth's tranquil light;
And smothered joys into new being start.
From her unworthy seat, the cloudy stall
Of Time, breaks forth triumphant Memory;
Her glistening tresses bound, yet light and free
As golden locks of birch, that rise and fall
On gales that breathe too gently to recall
Aught of the fading year's inclemency!

"The River Duddon Sonnets", XXI.

1820

William Cobbett
[The oak on Tilford Green]

Our ... road was right over the heath through *Tilford* to *Farnham*; but
we veered a little to the left after we came to Tilford, at which place on the
Green we stopped to look at an *oak tree*, which, when I was a little boy,
was but a very little tree, comparatively, and which is now, take it altogether, by far the finest tree that I ever saw in my life. The stem or shaft is
short; that is today, it is short before you come to the first limbs; but it is
full *thirty feet round,* at about eight or ten feet from the ground. Out of

110

THENOT.

THENOT.

COLINET.

COLINET.

William Blake, wood engravings for the first "Eclogue"
in Robert John Thornton's Virgil.

1821

the stem there come not less than fifteen or sixteen limbs, many of which are from five to ten feet round, and each of which would, in fact, be considered a decent stick of timber. I am not judge enough of timber to say anything about the quantity in the whole tree, but my son stepped the ground, and as nearly as we could judge, the diameter of the extent of the branches was upwards of ninety feet, which would make a circumference of about three hundred feet. The tree is in full growth at this moment. There is a little hole in one of the limbs; but with that exception, there appears not the smallest sign of decay. The tree has made great shoots in all parts of it this last summer and spring; and there are no appearances of *white* upon the trunk, such as are regarded as the symptoms of full growth. There are many sorts of oak in England; two very distinct: one with a pale leaf, and one with a dark leaf: this is of the pale leaf. The tree stands upon Tilford-green, the soil of which is a light loam with a hard sand stone a good way beneath, and, probably, clay beneath that. The spot where the tree stands is about a hundred and twenty feet from the edge of a little river, and the ground on which it stands may be about ten feet higher than the bed of that river.

From *Rural Rides.*

27 September 1822

∾

George Gordon, Lord Byron

["Where the Druid oak / Stood like Caractacus"]

To Norman Abbey whirled the noble pair, –
　An old, old Monastery once, and now
Still older mansion – of a rich and rare
　Mixed Gothic, such as artists all allow
Few specimens yet left us can compare
　Withal: it lies, perhaps, a little low,
Because the monks preferred a hill behind,
To shelter their devotion from the wind.

It stood embosomed in a happy valley,
    Crowned by high woodlands, where the Druid oak
Stood like Caractacus, in act to rally
    His host, with broad arms 'gainst the thunder-stroke;
And from beneath his boughs were seen to sally
    The dappled foresters, as Day awoke,
The branching stag swept down with all his herd,
To quaff a brook which murmured like a bird.

Before the mansion lay a lucid Lake,
    Broad as transparent, deep, and freshly fed
By a river, which its softened way did take
    In currents through the calmer water spread
Around: the wildfowl nestled in the brake
    And sedges, brooding in their liquid bed:
The woods sloped downwards to its brink, and stood
With their green faces fixed upon the flood.

Its outlet dashed into a deep cascade,
    Sparkling with foam, until again subsiding,
Its shriller echoes – like an infant made
    Quiet – sank into softer ripples, gliding
Into a rivulet; and thus allayed,
    Pursued its course, now gleaming, and now hiding
Its windings through the woods; now clear, now blue,
According as the skies their shadows threw.

From *Don Juan*, XIII.

1823

"Landscape with Figure Embracing a Tree," by Samuel Palmer.

Private collection.

ca. 1827

Walter Savage Landor
["The only things that money cannot command"]

Old trees in their living state are the only things that money cannot command. Rivers leave their beds, run into cities, and traverse mountains for it; obelisks and arches, palaces and temples, amphitheatres and pyramids, rise up like exhalations at its bidding; even the free spirit of Man, the only thing great on earth, crouches and cowers in its presence. It passes away and vanishes before venerable trees.

From *Imaginary Conversations*, Italian XIX.

1824

Oliver Wendell Holmes
["A venerable relic of the Revolution"]

I saw him once before,
As he passed by the door,
    And again
The pavement stones resound,
As he totters o'er the ground
    With his cane.

They say that in his prime,
Ere the pruning-knife of Time
    Cut him down,
Not a better man was found
By the Crier on his round
    Through the town.

. . . .

"The Seven Sisters" in 1830.
From *Old and New London*, ca. 1875.

I know it is a sin
For me to sit and grin
    At him here;
But the old three-cornered hat,
And the breeches, and all that,
    Are so queer!

And if I should live to be
The last leaf upon the tree
    In the spring,
Let them smile, as I do now
At the old forsaken bough
    Where I cling.

From "The Last Leaf".

1831

∾

Nathaniel Hawthorne
["The haunted forest"]

"My Faith is gone!" cried he, after one stupefied moment. "There is no good on earth; and sin is but a name. Come, devil; for to thee is this world given."

And, maddened with despair, so that he laughed loud and long, did Goodman Brown grasp his staff and set forth again, at such a rate that he seemed to fly along the forest path rather than to walk or run. The road grew wilder and drearier and more faintly traced, and vanished at length, leaving him in the heart of the dark wilderness, still rushing onward with the instinct that guides mortal man to evil. The whole forest was peopled with frightful sounds – the creaking of the trees, the howling of wild beasts, and the yells of Indians; while sometimes the wind tolled like a distant church bell, and sometimes gave a broad roar around the traveller, as if all Nature were laughing him to scorn. But he was himself the chief horror of the scene, and shrank not from its other horrors.

"Ha! ha! ha!" roared Goodman Brown when the wind laughed at him. "Let us hear which will laugh loudest. Think not to frighten me with your deviltry. Come witch, come wizard, come Indian pow-wow, come devil himself, and here comes Goodman Brown. You may as well fear him as he fear you."

In truth, all through the haunted forest there could be nothing more frightful than the figure of Goodman Brown. On he flew among the black pines, brandishing his staff with frenzied gestures, now giving vent to an inspiration of horrid blasphemy, and now shouting forth such laughter as set all the echoes of the forest laughing like demons around him. The fiend in his own shape is less hideous than when he rages in the breast of man. Thus sped the demoniac on his course, until, quivering among the trees, he saw a red light before him, as when the felled trunks and branches of a clearing have been set on fire, and throw up their lurid blaze against the sky, at the hour of midnight. He paused, in a lull of the tempest that had driven him onward, and heard the swell of what seemed a hymn, rolling solemnly from a distance with the weight of many voices. He knew the tune; it was a familiar one in the choir of the village meeting-house. The verse died heavily away, and was lengthened by a chorus, not of human voices, but of all the sounds of the benighted wilderness pealing in awful harmony together. Goodman Brown cried out, and his cry was lost to his own ear by its unison with the cry of the desert.

In the interval of silence he stole forward until the light glared full upon his eyes. At one extremity of an open space, hemmed in by the dark wall of the forest, arose a rock, bearing some rude, natural resemblance either to an altar or a pulpit, and surrounded by four blazing pines, their tops aflame, their stems untouched, like candles at an evening meeting. The mass of foliage that had overgrown the summit of the rock was all on fire, blazing high into the night and fitfully illuminating the whole field. Each pendant twig and leafy festoon was in a blaze. As the red light arose and fell, a numerous congregation alternately shone forth, then disappeared in shadow, and again grew, as it were, out of the darkness, peopling the heart of the solitary woods at once.

"A grave and dark-clad company," quoth Goodman Brown.

In truth they were such. Among them, quivering to and fro between gloom and splendor, appeared faces that would be seen next day at the council board of the province, and others which, Sabbath after Sabbath, looked devoutly heavenward, and benignantly over the crowded pews, from the holiest pulpits in the land.

From "Young Goodman Brown".

1835

Thomas Campbell
The Beech Tree's Petition

O leave this barren spot to me!
Spare, woodman, spare the beechen tree!
Though bush or flow'ret never grow
My dark unwarming shade below;
Nor summer bud perfume the dew
Of rosy blush, or yellow hue!
Nor fruits of autumn, blossom-born,
My green and glossy leaves adorn;
Nor murmuring tribes from me derive
Th' ambrosial amber of the hive;
Yet leave this barren spot to me;
Spare, woodman, spare the beechen tree!

Thrice twenty summers I have seen
The sky grow bright, the forest green;
And many a wintry wind have stood
In bloomless, fruitless solitude,
Since childhood in my pleasant bower
First spent its sweet and sportive hour,

J. M. W. Turner, "The Beech Tree's Petition."
Engraved by Edward Goodall,
for Thomas Campbell's Poetical Works.
1837

Since youthful lovers in my shade
Their vows of truth and rapture made;
And on my trunk's surviving frame
Carved many a long-forgotten name.
Oh! by the sighs of gentle sound,
First breathe upon this sacred ground;
By all that Love has whisper'd here,
Or Beauty heard with ravish'd ear;
As Love's own altar honor me:
Spare, woodman, spare the beechen tree!

1837

Anna Brownell Jameson
[Forest Trees in Canada]

At Hamilton I hired a light *wagon,* as they call it, a sort of gig perched in the middle of a wooden tray, wherein my baggage was stowed; and a man to drive me over to Brandtford, the distance being about five-and-twenty miles, and the charge five dollars. The country all the way was rich, and beautiful, and fertile beyond description – the roads as abominable as could be imagined to exist....I remember a space of about three miles on this road, bordered entirely on each side by dead trees, which had been artificially blasted by fire, or by girdling. It was a ghastly forest of tall white spectres, strangely contrasting with the glowing luxurious foliage all around.

The pity I have for the trees of Canada, shows how far I am yet from being a true Canadian.... Without exactly believing the assertion of the old philosopher, that a tree *feels* the first stoke of the axe, I know I never witness nor hear that first stroke without a shudder; and as yet I cannot look on with indifference, far less share the Canadian's exultation, when these huge oaks, these umbrageous elms and stately pines, are lying prostrate, lopped of all their honours, and piled in heaps with the brushwood, to be fired, – or burned down to a charred and blackened fragment, – or standing, leafless, sapless, seared, ghastly, having been "girdled," and left to perish. The "Fool i' the Forest," moralised not more quaintly over the wounded deer, than I could sometimes over those prostrated and mangled trees. I remember, in one of the clearings to-day, one particular tree which had been burned and blasted; only a blackened stump of mouldering bark – a mere shell remained; and from the centre of this, as from some hidden source of vitality, sprang up a young green shoot, tall and flourishing, and fresh and leafy. I looked and thought of hope! Why, indeed, should we ever despair? Can Heaven do for the blasted tree what it cannot do for the human heart?

....

No one who has a single atom of imagination, can travel through these forest roads of Canada without being strongly impressed and excited. The seemingly interminable line of trees before you; the boundless wilderness around; the mysterious depths among the multitudinous foliage, where foot of man never penetrated, – and which partial gleams of the noontide sun, now seen, now lost, lit up with a changeful, magical beauty – the wondrous splendour and novelty of the flowers, – the silence, unbroken but by the low cry of a bird, or hum of insect, or the splash and croak of some huge bull-frog, – the solitude in which we proceeded mile after mile, no human being, no human dwelling within sight, – are all either exciting to the fancy, or oppressive to the spirits, according to the mood one may be in. Their effect on myself I can hardly describe in words.

From *Winter Studies and Summer Rambles in Canada.*

1837

❧

James Fenimore Cooper

["The vastness of the view"]

The sublimity connected with vastness, is familiar to every eye. The most abstruse, the most far-reaching, perhaps the most chastened of the poet's thoughts, crowd on the imagination as he gazes into the depths of the illimitable void; the expanse of ocean is seldom seen by the novice, with indifference, and the mind, even in the obscurity of night, finds a parallel to that grandeur, which seems inseparable from images that the senses cannot compass. With feelings akin to this admiration and awe, the offspring of sublimity, were the different characters with which the action of this tale must open, gazing on the scene before them. Four persons in all, two of each sex, they had managed to ascend a pile of trees, that had been uptorn by a tempest, to catch a view of the objects that surrounded them. It is still the practice of the country to call these spots wind-rows. By letting in the light of heaven upon the dark and damp recesses of the wood, they form a sort of oases in the solemn obscurity of the virgin forests of America. The particular wind-row of which we are writing lay on the brow of a gentle acclivity, and it had opened the way for an extensive view.... On the upper margin of the opening...the viewless influence had piled tree on tree in such a manner as had not only enabled the two males of the party to ascend to an elevation of some thirty feet above the level of the earth, but, with a little care and encouragement, to induce their more timid companions to accompany them. The vast trunks, that had been broken and riven by the force of the gust, lay blended like jack-straws, while their branches, still exhaling the fragrance of wilted leaves, were interlaced in a manner to afford sufficient support to the hands. One tree had been completely uprooted, and its lower end, filled with earth, had been cast uppermost, in a way to supply a sort of staging for the four adventurers, when they had gained the desired distance from the ground.

... Two of the party, indeed, a male and known female, belonged to the native owners of the soil, being Indians of the well known tribe of the Tuscaroras, while their companions were a man, who bore about him the peculiarities of one who had passed his days on the ocean, and that, too, in a station little if any above that of a common mariner, while his female associate was a maiden of a class, in no great degree superior to his own, though her youth, sweetness of countenance, and a modest but spirited mien, lent that character of intellect and refinement, which adds so much to the charm of beauty, in the sex. On the present occasion, her full blue eye reflected the feeling of sublimity that the scene excited, and her pleasant face was beaming with the pensive expression, with which all deep emotions, even though they bring the most grateful pleasure, shadow the countenance of the ingenuous and thoughtful.

And, truly, the scene was of a nature, deeply to impress the imagination of the beholder. Towards the west, in which direction the faces of the party were turned, and in which alone could much be seen, the eye ranged over an ocean of leaves, glorious and rich in the varied but lively verdure of a generous vegetation, and shaded by the luxuriant tints that belong to the forty-second degree of latitude. The elm, with its graceful and sweeping top, the rich varieties of the maple, most of the noble oaks of the American forest, with the broad-leafed linden, known in the parlance of the country as the bass-wood, mingled their uppermost branches, forming one broad and seemingly interminable carpet of foliage, that stretched away towards the setting sun until it bounded the horizon, by blending with the clouds, as the waves and the sky meet at the base of the vault of Heaven. Here and there, by some accident of the tempests, or by a caprice of nature, a trifling opening among these giant members of the forest, permitted an inferior tree to struggle upward toward the light, and to lift its modest head nearly to a level with the surrounding surface of verdure. Of this class were the birch, a tree of some account, in regions less favored, the quivering aspen, various generous nut-woods, and divers others, that resembled the ignoble and vulgar, thrown by circumstances, into the presence of the stately and great. Here and there, too, the tall, straight trunk of the pine, pierced the vast field, rising high above it, like some grand monument reared by art on a plain of leaves.

It was the vastness of the view, the nearly unbroken surface of verdure, that contained the principle of grandeur. The beauty was to be traced in the delicate tints, relieved by gradations of light and shadow, while the solemn repose, induced a feeling allied to awe.

From *The Pathfinder*, I.

1840

George P. Morris
Woodman, Spare That Tree

Woodman, spare that tree!
    Touch not a single bough!
In youth it sheltered me,
    And I'll protect it now.
'Twas my forefather's hand
    That plac'd it near his cot;
There, woodman, let it stand,
    Thy axe shall harm it not!

That old familiar tree,
    Whose glory and renown
Are spread o'er land and sea,
    And wouldst thou hew it down?
Woodman, forbear thy stroke!
    Cut not its earth-bound ties;
O, spare that aged oak,
    Now towering to the skies!

When but an idle boy
    I sought its grateful shade;
In all their gushing joy
    Here too my sisters played.
My mother kissed me here;
    My father pressed my hand –
Forgive this foolish tear,
    But let that old oak stand!

My heart-strings round thee cling,
    Close as thy bark, old friend!
Here shall the wild-bird sing,
    And still thy branches bend.
Old tree! the storm still brave!
    And, woodman, leave the spot;
While I've a hand to save,
    Thy axe shall hurt it not.

ca. 1840

Charles Dickens
["Monotonous desolation"]

At first they parted with some of their passengers once or twice a day, and took in others to replace them. But by degrees the towns upon their route became more thinly scattered; and for many hours together they would see no other habitations than the huts of the wood-cutters, where the vessel stopped for fuel. Sky, wood, and water, all the livelong day; and heat that blistered everything it touched.

On they toiled through great solitudes, where the trees upon the banks grew thick and close; and floated in the stream; and held up shrivelled arms from out the river's depths; and slid down from the margin of the land: half growing, half decaying, in the miry water. On through the weary day and melancholy night: beneath the burning sun, and in the mist and vapour of the evening: on, until return appeared impossible, and restoration to their home a miserable dream.

They had now but few people on board, and these few were as flat, as dull and stagnant, as the vegetation that oppressed their eyes. No sound of cheerfulness or hope was heard; no pleasant talk beguiled the tardy time; no little group made common cause against the dull depression of the scene. But that, at certain periods, they swallowed food together from

View in Greenwich Park.

From *Old and New London*, ca. 1875.

a common trough, it might have been old Charon's boat, conveying melancholy shades to judgment.

....

As they proceeded further on their track, and came more and more towards their journey's end, the monotonous desolation of the scene increased to that degree, that for any redeeming feature it presented to their eyes, they might have entered, in the body, on the grim domains of Giant Despair. A flat morass bestrewn with fallen timber; a marsh on which the good growth of the earth seemed to have been wrecked and cast away, that from its decomposing ashes vile and ugly things might rise; where the very trees took the aspect of huge weeds, begotten of the slime from which they sprung, by the hot sun that burnt them up; where fatal maladies, seeking whom they might infect, came forth at night, in misty shapes, and creeping out upon the water, hunted them like spectres until day; where even the blessed sun, shining down on festering elements of corruption and disease, became a horror; this was the realm of Hope through which they moved.

At last they stopped. At Eden too. The waters of the Deluge might have left it but a week before: so choked with slime and matted growth was the hideous swamp which bore that name.

From *Martin Chuzzlewit*, XXIII.

1843

Edward Lear

["There was an old man in a tree"]

There was an old man in a tree,
Whose whiskers were lovely to see;
But the birds of the air, pluck'd them perfectly bare,
To make themselves nests in that tree.

---

ca. 1846

&

Henry Wadsworth Longfellow
["This is the forest primeval"]

This is the forest primeval. The murmuring pines and the hemlocks,
Bearded with moss, and in garments green, indistinct in the twilight,
Stand like Druids of eld, with voices sad and prophetic,
Stand like harpers hoar, with beards that rest on their bosoms.
Loud from its rocky caverns, the deep-voiced neighboring ocean
Speaks, and in accents disconsolate answers the wail of the forest.

This is the forest primeval; but where are the hearts that beneath it
Leaped like the roe, when he hears in the woodland the voice of the
     huntsman?
Where is the thatch-roofed village, the home of Acadian farmers, –
Men whose lives glided on like rivers that water the woodlands,
Darkened by shadows of earth, but reflecting an image of heaven?
Waste are those pleasant farms, and the farmers forever departed!
Scattered like dust and leaves, when the mighty blasts of October
Seize them, and whirl them aloft, and sprinkle them far o'er the ocean.
Naught but tradition remains of the beautiful village of Grand-Pré.

Ye who believe in affection that hopes, and endures, and is patient,
Ye who believe in the beauty and strength of woman's devotion,
List to the mournful tradition, still sung by the pines of the forest;
List to a Tale of Love in Acadie, home of the happy.

From *Evangeline*, Introduction.

1847

James O. Halliwell-Phillipps
The Oxford Student

Many years ago there lived at the University of Oxford a young student, who, having seduced the daughter of a tradesman, sought to conceal his crime by committing the more heinous one of murder. With this view, he made an appointment to meet her one evening in a secluded field. She was at the rendezvous considerably before the time agreed upon for their meeting, and hid herself in a tree. The student arrived on the spot shortly afterwards, but what was the astonishment of the girl to observe that he commenced digging a grave. Her fears and suspicions were aroused, and she did not leave her place of concealment till the student, despairing of her arrival, returned to his college. The next day, when she was at the door of her father's house, he passed and saluted her as usual. She returned his greeting by repeating the following lines:

> One moonshiny night, as I sat high,
> Waiting for one to come by,
> The boughs did bend; my heart did ache,
> To see what hole the fox did make.

Astounded by her unexpected knowledge of his base design, in a moment of fury he stabbed her to the heart. This murder occasioned a violent conflict between the tradespeople and the students, the latter taking part with the murderer, and so fierce was the skirmish, that Brewer's Lane, it is said, ran down with blood. The place of appointment was adjoining the Divinity Walk, which was in time past far more secluded than at the present day, and she is said to have been buried in the grave made for her by her paramour.

From *Popular Rhymes and Nursery Tales.*

1849

~

Alfred, Lord Tennyson
[The old yew]

Old Yew, which graspest at the stones
  That name the under-lying dead,
  Thy fibres net the dreamless head,
Thy roots are wrapt about the bones.

The seasons bring the flower again,
  And bring the firstling to the flock;
  And in the dusk of thee, the clock
Beats out the little lives of men.

O not for thee the glow, the bloom,
  Who changest not in any gale,
  Nor branding summer suns avail
To touch thy thousand years of gloom:

And gazing on thee, sullen tree,
  Sick for thy stubborn hardihood,
  I seem to fail from out my blood
And grow incorporate into thee.

———————

In Memoriam, II.

1850

William Westall, "Crosthwaite Church from Greta Hall [Robert Southey's home in Keswick]." Engraved by E. Finden.

1850

Susanna Moodie
["A logging-bee"]

A logging-bee followed the burning of the fallow as a matter of course. In the bush, where hands are few and labour commands an enormous rate of wages, these gatherings are considered indispensable, and much has been written in their praise; but to me, they present the most disgusting picture of a bush life. They are noisy, riotous, drunken meetings, often terminating in violent quarrels, sometimes even in bloodshed. Accidents of the most serious nature often occur, and very little work is done when we consider the number of hands employed, and the great consumption of food and liquor.

....

People in the woods have a craze for giving and going to bees, and run to them with as much eagerness as a peasant runs to a racecourse or a fair; plenty of strong drink and excitement making the chief attraction of the bee.

....

Thirty-two men, gentle and simple, were invited to our bee, and the maid and I were engaged for two days preceding the important one, in baking and cooking for the entertainment of our guests. When I looked at the quantity of food we had prepared, I thought that it never could be all eaten, even by thirty-two men. It was a burning hot day towards the end of July when our loggers began to come in, and the "gee!" and "ha!" to encourage the oxen resounded on every side.

....

Our men worked well until dinner-time, when, after washing in the lake, they all sat down to the rude board which I had prepared for them, loaded with the best fare that could be procured in the bush. Pea-soup, legs of pork, venison, eel, and raspberry pies, garnished with plenty of potatoes, and whiskey to wash them down, besides a large iron kettle of tea. To pour out the latter, and dispense it round, devolved upon me. My brother and his friends, who were all temperance men, and consequently the best workers in the field, kept me and the maid actively employed in replenishing their cups.

The dinner passed off tolerably well; some of the lower order of the Irish settlers were pretty far gone, but they committed no outrage upon our feelings by either swearing or bad language, a few harmless jokes alone circulating among them.

....

After the sun went down, the logging-band came in to supper, which was all ready for them. Those who remained sober ate the meal in peace, and quietly returned to their own homes, while the vicious and the drunken stayed to brawl and fight.

After having placed the supper on the table, I was so tired with the noise, and heat, and fatigue of the day, that I went to bed, leaving to Mary and my husband the care of the guests.

The little bed-chamber was only separated from the kitchen by a few thin boards; and, unfortunately for me and the girl, who was soon forced to retreat thither, we could hear all the wickedness and profanity going on in the next room. My husband, disgusted with the scene, soon left it, and retired into the parlour with the few of the loggers who, at that hour, re-mained sober. The house rang with the sound of unhallowed revelry, pro-fane songs, and blasphemous swearing. It would have been no hard task to have imagined these miserable, degraded beings, fiends instead of men. How glad I was when they at last broke up and we were once more left in peace to collect the broken glasses and cups, and the scattered frag-ments of that hateful feast!

We were obliged to endure a second and a third repetition of this odi-ous scene, before sixteen acres of land were rendered fit for the reception for our fall crop of wheat.

From *Roughing it in the Bush*, XIII.

1852

Henry Thoreau

["The shrines I visited"]

Sometimes I rambled to pine groves, standing like temples, or like fleets at sea, full-rigged, with wavy boughs, and rippling with light, so soft and green and shady that the Druids would have forsaken their oaks to worship in them; or to the cedar wood beyond Flint's Pond, where the trees, covered with hoary blue berries, spiring higher and higher, are fit to stand before Valhalla, and the creeping juniper covers the ground with wreaths full of fruit; or to swamps where the usnea lichen hangs in festoons from the black-spruce trees, and toad-stools, round tables of the swamp gods, cover the ground, and more beautiful fungi adorn the stumps, like butterflies or shells, vegetable winkles; where the swamp-pink and dogwood grow, the red alder-berry glows like eyes of imps, the waxwork grooves and crushes the hardest woods in its folds, and the wild-holly berries make the beholder forget his home with their beauty, and he is dazzled and tempted by nameless other wild forbidden fruits, too fair for mortal taste. Instead of calling on some scholar, I paid many a visit to particular trees, of kinds which are rare in this neighborhood, standing far away in the middle of some pasture, or in the depths of a wood or swamp, or on a hill-top; such as the black-birch, of which we have some handsome specimens two feet in diameter; its cousin the yellow-birch, with its loose golden vest, perfumed like the first; the beech, which has so neat a bole and beautifully lichen-painted, perfect in all its details, of which, excepting scattered specimens, I know but one small grove of sizeable trees left in the township, supposed by some to have been planted by the pigeons that were once baited with beech nuts near by; it is worth the while to see the silver grain sparkle when you split this wood; the bass; the hornbeam; the *Celtis occidentalis*, or false elm, of which we have but one well-grown; some taller mast of a pine, a shingle tree, or a more perfect hemlock than usual, standing like a pagoda in the midst of the woods; and many others I could mention. These were the shrines I visited both summer and winter.

From *Walden, or Life in the Woods.*

1854

✦

Thomas Bulfinch
[Ygdrasill]

Odin then regulated the periods of day and night and the seasons by placing in the heavens the sun and moon and appointing to them their respective courses. As soon as the sun began to shed its rays upon the earth, it caused the vegetable world to bud and sprout. Shortly after the gods had created the world they walked by the side of the sea, pleased with their new work, but found that it was still incomplete, for it was without human beings. They therefore took an ash tree and made a man out of it, and they made a woman out of an elder, and called the man Aske and the woman Embla. Odin then gave them life and soul, Vili reason and motion, and Ve bestowed upon them the senses, expressive features, and speech. Midgard was then given them as their residence, and they became the progenitors of the human race.

The mighty ash tree Ygdrasill was supposed to support the whole universe. It sprang from the body of Ymir, and had three immense roots, extending one into Asgard (the dwelling of the gods), the other into Jotunheim (the abode of the giants), and the third to Niffleheim (the regions of darkness and cold). By the side of each of these roots is a spring, from which it is watered. The root that extends into Asgard is carefully tended by the three Norns, goddesses, who are regarded as the dispensers of fate. They are Urdur (the past), Verdandi (the present), Skuld (the future). The spring at the Jotunheim side is Ymir's well, in which wisdom and wit lie hidden, but that of Niffleheim feeds the adder Nidhogge (darkness), which perpetually gnaws at the root. Four harts run across the branches of the tree and bite the buds; they represent the four winds. Under the tree lies Ymir, and when he tries to shake off its weight the earth quakes.

From Bulfinch's Mythology.

1855

Walt Whitman

I Saw in Louisiana a Live-Oak Growing

I saw in Louisiana a live-oak growing,
All alone it stood and the moss hung down from the branches,
Without any companion it grew there uttering joyous leaves of dark green,
And its look, rude, unbending, lusty, made me think of myself,
But I wonder'd how it could utter joyous leaves standing alone there
    without its friend near, for I knew I could not,
And I broke off a twig with a certain number of leaves upon it, and
    twined around it a little moss,
And brought it away, and I have placed it in sight in my room,
It is not needed to remind me as of my own dear friends,
(For I believe lately I think of little else than of them),
Yet it remains to me a curious token, it makes me think of manly love;
For all that, and though the live-oak glistens there in Louisiana solitary
    in a wide flat space,
Uttering joyous leaves all its life without a friend a lover near,
I know very well I could not.

1855

John Ruskin

[Classical, Medieval, and Modern Attitudes Towards Trees]

But to return more definitely to our Homeric landscape. When it is perfect, we have, as in the above instances, the foliage and meadows together; when imperfect, it is always either the foliage or the meadow; preeminently the meadow, or arable field.... In this same passage [*Odyssey*, V], also, we find some peculiar expressions of the delight which the Greeks had in trees; for, when Ulysses first comes in sight of land, which gladdens him 'as the reviving of a father from his sickness gladdens his children,' it is not merely the sight of the land itself which gives him such pleasure, but of the 'land and *wood*.' Homer never throws away any words, at least in such a place as this; and what in another poet would have been merely the filling up of the deficient line with an otherwise useless word, is in him the expression of the general Greek sense, that land of any kind was in nowise grateful or acceptable till there was *wood* upon it (or corn; but the corn, in the flats, could not be seen so far as the black masses of forest on the hill sides), and that, as in being rushy and corn-giving, the low land, so in being woody, the high land was most grateful to the mind of the man who for days and nights had been wearied on the engulphing sea. And this general idea of wood and corn, as the types of the fatness of the whole earth, is beautifully marked in another place of the *Odyssey* [XII], where the sailors in a desert island, having no flour of corn to offer as a meat offering with their sacrifices, take the leaves of the trees, and scatter them over the burnt offering instead.

But still, every expression of the pleasure which Ulysses has in this landing and resting, contains uninterruptedly the reference to the utility and sensible pleasantness of all things, not to their beauty. After his first grateful kiss given to the corn-growing land, he considers immediately how he is to pass the night; for some minutes hesitating whether it will be best to expose himself to the misty chill from the river, or run the risk of wild beasts in the wood. He decides for the wood, and finds in it a bower formed by a sweet and a wild olive tree, interlacing their branches, or – perhaps more accurately translating Homer's intensely graphic expression – 'changing their branches with each other' (it is very curious how often, in an entanglement of wood, one supposes the branches to belong to the wrong trees) and forming a roof penetrated by neither rain, sun, nor wind. Under this bower Ulysses collects the '*vain* (or *frustrate*) outpouring of the dead leaves' – another exquisite expression, used elsewhere of useless grief or shedding of tears; – and, having got enough together, makes his bed of them, and goes to sleep, having covered himself up with them, 'as embers are covered up with ashes.'

Nothing can possibly be more intensely possessive of the *facts* than this whole passage; the sense of utter deadness and emptiness, and frustrate fall in the leaves; of dormant life in the human body, – the fire, and heroism, and strength of it, lulled under the dead brown heap, as embers under ashes, and the knitting of interchanged and close strength of living boughs above. But there is not the smallest apparent sense of there being *beauty* elsewhere than in the human being. The wreathed wood is admired simply as being a perfect roof for it; the fallen leaves only as being a perfect bed for it; and there is literally no more excitement of emotion in Homer, as he describes them, nor does he expect us to be more excited or touched by hearing about them, than if he had been telling us how the chamber-maid at the Bull aired the four-poster, and put on two extra blankets.

....

In our examination of the spirit of classical landscape, we were obliged to confine ourselves to what is left to us in written description. Some interesting results might indeed have been obtained by examining the Egyptian and Ninevite landscape sculpture, but in nowise conclusive enough to be worth the pains of the inquiry; for the landscape of sculpture is necessarily confined in range, and usually inexpressive of the complete feelings of the workman, being introduced rather to explain the place and circumstances of events, than for its own sake. In the Middle Ages, however, the case is widely different. We have written landscape, sculptured landscape, and painted landscape, all bearing united testimony to the tone of the national mind in almost every remarkable locality of Europe.

That testimony, taken in its breadth, is very curiously conclusive. It marks the mediaeval mind as agreeing altogether with the ancients, in holding that flat land, brooks, and groves of aspens, compose the pleasant places of the earth, and that rocks and mountains are, for inhabitation, altogether to be reprobated and detested; but as disagreeing with the classical mind totally in this other most important respect, that the pleasant flat land is never a ploughed field, nor a rich lotus meadow good for pasture, but *garden* ground covered with flowers, and divided by fragrant hedges, with a castle in the middle of it. The aspens are delighted in, not because they are good for 'coach-making men' to make cart-wheels of, but because they are shady and graceful; and the fruit-trees, covered with delicious fruit, especially apple and orange, occupy still more important positions in the scenery. Singing-birds – not 'sea-crows,' but nightingales – perch on every bough; and the ideal occupation of mankind is not to cultivate either the garden or the meadow, but to gather roses and eat oranges in the one, and ride out hawking over the other.

....

Such, then, being the weaknesses which it was necessary that [Sir Walter] Scott should share with his age, in order that he might sufficiently represent it, and such the grounds for supposing him, in spite of all these weaknesses, the greatest literary man whom that age produced, let us glance at the principal points in which his view of landscape differs from that of the mediaevals....

And, first, observe Scott's habit of looking at nature neither as dead, or merely material, in the way that Homer regards it, nor as altered by his own feelings, in the way that Keats and Tennyson regard it, but as having an animation and pathos of *its own*, wholly irrespective of human presence or passion, – an animation which Scott loves and sympathizes with, as he would with a fellow creature, forgetting himself altogether, and subduing his own humanity before what seems to him the power of the landscape.

> 'Yon lonely thorn, – would he could tell
> The changes of his parent dell,
> Since he, so grey and stubborn now,
> Waved in each breeze a sapling bough!
> Would he could tell, how deep the shade
> A thousand mingled branches made,
> How broad the shadows of the oak,
> How clung the rowan to the rock,
> And through the foliage showed his head,
> With narrow leaves and berries red!'
> [*Marmion*, Canto II, Introduction]

Scott does not dwell on the grey stubbornness of the thorn, because he himself is at that moment disposed to be dull, or stubborn; neither on the cheerful peeping forth of the rowan, because he himself is at that moment cheerful or curious: but he perceives them both with the kind of interest that he would take in an old man, or a climbing boy; forgetting himself, in sympathy with either age or youth.

From *Modern Painters*, Vol. III, Part IV, Chaps. xiii, xiv, xvi.

1856

❧

Elizabeth Barrett Browning
["A sweet familiar nature"]

I had a little chamber in the house,
As green as any privet-hedge a bird
Might choose to build in, though the nest itself
Could show but dead-brown sticks and straws; the walls
Were green, the carpet was pure green, the straight
Small bed was curtained greenly, and the folds
Hung green about the window, which let in
The out-door world with all its greenery.
You could not push your head out and escape
A dash of dawn-dew from the honeysuckle,
But so you were baptized into the grace
And privilege of seeing....

                    First, the lime
(I had enough, there, of the lime, be sure, –
My morning-dream was often hummed away
By the bees in it); past the lime, the lawn,
Which, after sweeping broadly round the house,
Went trickling through the shrubberies in a stream
Of tender turf, and wore and lost itself
Among the acacias, over which, you saw
The irregular line of elms by the deep lane
Which stopped the grounds and dammed the overflow
Or arbutus and laurel. Out of sight
The lane was; sunk so deep, no foreign tramp
Nor drover of wild ponies out of Wales
Could guess if lady's hall or tenant's lodge
Dispensed such odours, – though his stick well-crook'd
Might reach the lowest trail of blossoming briar
Which dipped upon the wall. Behind the elms,
And through their tops, you saw the folded hills
Striped up and down with hedges (burly oaks

Projecting from the lines to show themselves),
Through which my cousin Romney's chimneys smoked
As still as when a silent mouth in frost
Breathes – showing where the woodlands hid Leigh Hall;
While, far above, a jut of table-land,
A promontory without water, stretched, –
You could not catch it if the days were thick,
Or took it for a cloud; but, otherwise
The vigorous sun would catch it up at eve
And use it for an anvil till he had filled
The shelves of heaven with burning thunderbolts,
And proved he need not rest so early: – then,
When all his setting trouble was resolved
To a trance of passive glory, you might see
In apparition on the golden sky
(Alas, my Giotto's background!) the sheep run
Along the fine clear outline, small as mice
That run along a witch's scarlet thread.

Not a grand nature. Not my chestnut-woods
Of Vallombrosa, cleaving by the spurs
To the precipices. Not my headlong leaps
Of waters, that cry out for joy or fear
In leaping through the palpitating pines,
Like a white soul tossed out to eternity
With thrills of time upon it. Not indeed
My multitudinous mountains, sitting in
The magic circle, with the mutual touch
Electric, panting from their full deep hearts
Beneath the influent heavens, and waiting for
Communion and commission. Italy
Is one thing, England one.
                              On English ground
You understand the letter…ere the fall,
How Adam lived in a garden. All the fields
Are tied up fast with hedges, nosegay-like;

The hills are crumpled plains, – the plains, parterres, –
The trees, round, woolly, ready to be clipped;
And if you seek for any wilderness
You find, at best, a park. A nature tamed
And grown domestic like a barn-door fowl,
Which does not awe you with its claws and beak,
Nor tempt you to an eyrie too high up,
But which, in cackling, sets you thinking of
Your eggs to-morrow at breakfast, in the pause
Of finer meditation.
              Rather say,
A sweet familiar nature, stealing in
As a dog might, or child, to touch your hand
Or pluck your gown, and humbly mind you so
Of presence and affection, excellent
For inner uses, from the things without.

From *Aurora Leigh*.
1857

‽

George Eliot
[Arthur Donnithorne meets Hetty]

Arthur's shadow flitted rather faster among the sturdy oaks of the Chase than might have been expected from the shadow of a tired man on a warm afternoon, and it was still scarcely four o'clock when he stood before the tall narrow gate leading into the delicious labyrinthine wood which skirted one side of the Chase, and which was called Fir-tree Grove, not because the firs were many, but because they were few. It was a wood of beeches and limes, with here and there a light, silver-stemmed birch – just the sort of wood most haunted by the nymphs: you see their white sunlit limbs gleaming athwart the boughs, or peeping from behind the smooth-sweeping outline of a tall lime; you hear their soft liquid laughter – but if you look with a too curious sacrilegious eye, they vanish behind the silvery beeches, they make you believe that their voice was only a running brooklet, perhaps they metamorphose themselves into a tawny squirrel that scampers away and mocks you from the topmost bough. It was not a grove with measured grass or rolled gravel for you to tread upon, but with narrow, hollow-shaped, earthy paths, edged with faint dashes of delicate moss – paths which look as if they were made by the free-will of the trees and underwood, moving reverently aside to look at the tall queen of the white-footed nymphs.

It was along the broadest of these paths that Arthur Donnithorne passed, under an avenue of limes and beeches. It was a still afternoon – the golden light was lingering languidly among the upper boughs, only glancing down here and there on the purple pathway and its edge of faintly-sprinkled moss: an afternoon in which destiny disguises her cold awful face behind a hazy radiant veil, encloses us in warm downy wings, and poisons us with violet-scented breath. Arthur strolled along carelessly, with a book under his arm, but not looking on the ground as meditative men are apt to do; his eyes *would* fix themselves on the distant bend in the road, round which a little figure must surely appear before long. Ah! there she comes: first a bright patch of colour, like a tropic bird among the boughs, then a tripping figure, with a round hat on, and a small basket under her arm, then a deep-blushing, almost frightened, but bright-smiling girl, making her curtsy with a fluttered yet happy glance, as Arthur came up to her.

From *Adam Bede*, XII.

1859

Birket Foster, [young woman with trees]. Vignette engraved by the Dalziels for the Poems of William Wordsworth.

1859

Wilkie Collins
[Scenes associated with the brief dream-time of happiness]

My hours were numbered at Limmeridge House; my departure the next morning was irrevocably settled; my share in the investigation which the anonymous letter had rendered necessary, was at an end. No harm could be done to anyone but myself, if I let my heart loose again, for the little time that was left me, from the cold cruelty of restraint which necessity had forced me to inflict upon it, and took my farewell of the scenes which were associated with the brief dream-time of my happiness and my love.

I turned instinctively to the walk beneath my study-window, where I had seen her the evening before with her little dog; and followed the path which her dear feet had trodden so often, till I came to the wicket gate that led into her rose garden. The winter bareness spread drearily over it, now. The flowers that she had taught me to distinguish by their names, the flowers that I had taught her to paint from, were gone; and the tiny white paths that led between the beds, were damp and green already. I went on to the avenue of trees, where we had breathed together the warm fragrance of August evenings; where we had admired together the myriad combinations of shade and sunlight that dappled the ground at our feet. The leaves fell about me from the groaning branches, and the earthy decay in the atmosphere chilled me to the bones. A little farther on, and I was out of the grounds, and following the lane that wound gently upward to the nearest hills. The old felled tree by the wayside, on which we had sat to rest, was sodden with rain; and the tuft of ferns and grasses which I had drawn for her, nestling under the rough stone wall in front of us, had turned to a pool of water stagnating round an island of draggled weeds. I gained the summit of the hill; and looked at the view which we had so often admired in the happier time. It was cold and barren – it was no longer the view that I remembered.

From "The [First] Narrative of Walter Hartright, of Clement's Inn,
London," *The Woman in White*, XIV.

1860

*Winslow Homer, [Northern picket in the Army of the Potomac,
American Civil War]. Woodcut,* Harper's Weekly.

15 November 1862

~

Benjamin Disraeli

["Talking to the people at work"]

I find great amusement in talking to the people at work in the woods & grounds at Hughenden. Their conversation is racy, & the repose of their natural manners agreeable....

I like very much the society of woodmen. Their conversation is most interesting – quick & constant observation, & perfect knowledge. I don't know any men, who are so completely masters of their business, & of the secluded, but delicious world in which they live. They are healthy. Their language is picturesque; they live in the air, & Nature whispers to them many of her secrets. A Forest, is like the Ocean, monotonous only to the ignorant. It is a life of ceaseless variety.

To see Lovett, my head-woodman fell a tree is a work of art. No bustle, no exertion, apparently not the slightest exercise of strength. He tickles it with his axe; & then it falls exactly where he desires it. He can climb a tree like a squirrel, an animal, which, both in form & color & expression, he seems to me to resemble.

From *Disraeli's Reminiscences*, VII.

1860

~

Col. G. F. R. Henderson

[The death of Stonewall Jackson]

Already his strength was fast ebbing, and although his face brightened when his baby was brought to him, his mind had begun to wander. Now he was on the battle-field, giving orders to his men; now at home in Lexington; now at prayers in the camp. Occasionally his senses came back to him, and about half-past one he was told that he had but two hours to live. Again he answered, feebly but firmly, "Very good; it is all right." These were almost his last coherent words. For some time he lay unconscious, and then suddenly he cried out: "Order A.P. Hill to prepare for action! Pass the infantry to the front! Tell Major Hawks – " then stopped, leaving the sentence unfinished. Once more he was silent; but a little while after he said very quietly and clearly, "Let us cross over the river, and rest under the shade of the trees," and the soul of the great captain passed into the peace of God.

From *Stonewall Jackson and the American Civil War*, II.

1863

⁓

Francis Parkman

[Cartier arrives at Hochelaga]

Slowly gliding on their way, by walls of verdure, brightened in the autumnal sun, they saw forests festooned with grape-vines, and waters alive with wild-fowl.... The galleon grounded; they left her, and, advancing with the boats alone, on the second of October [1535] neared the goal of their hopes, the mysterious Hochelaga.

Where now are seen the quays and storehouses of Montreal, a thousand Indians thronged the shore, wild with delight, dancing, singing, crowding about the strangers, and showering into the boats their gifts of fish and maize; and, as it grew dark, fires lighted up the night, while, far and near, the French could see the excited savages leaping and rejoicing by the blaze.

At dawn of day, marshalled and accoutred, they set forth for Hochelaga. An Indian path led them through the forest which covered the site of Montreal. The morning air was chill and sharp, the leaves were changing hue, and beneath the oaks the ground was thickly strewn with acorns. They soon met an Indian chief with a party of tribesmen, or, as the old narrative has it, "one of the principal lords of the said city," attended with a numerous retinue. Greeting them after the concise courtesy of the forest, he led them to a fire kindled by the side of the path for their comfort and refreshment, seated them on the earth, and made them a long harangue, receiving in requital of his eloquence two hatchets, two knives, and a crucifix, the last of which he was invited to kiss. This done, they resumed their march, and presently issued forth upon open fields, covered far and near with the ripened maize, its leaves rustling, its yellow grains gleaming between the parting husks. Before them, wrapped in forests painted by the early frosts, rose the ridgy back of the Mountain of Montreal, and below, encompassed with its cornfields, lay the Indian town. Nothing was visible but its encircling palisades. They were of trunks of trees, set in a triple row. The outer and inner ranges inclined till they met and crossed near the summit, while the upright row between them, aided by transverse braces, gave to the whole an abundant strength. Within were galleries for the defenders, rude ladders to mount them, and magazines of stones to throw down on the heads of assailants. It was a mode of fortification practised by all the tribes speaking dialects of the Iroquois.

From *Pioneers of France in the New World.*

1865

Francis Parkman

[Champlain arrives at Quebec]

It was on the eighteenth of September [1608] that Pontgravé set sail, leaving Champlain with twenty-eight men to hold Quebec through the winter. Three weeks later, and shores and hills glowed with gay prognostics of approaching desolation, – the yellow and scarlet of the maples, the deep purple of the ash, the garnet hue of young oaks, the crimson of the tupelo at the water's edge, and the golden plumage of birch saplings in the fissure of the cliff. It was a short-lived beauty. The forest dropped its festal robes. Shrivelled and faded, they rustled to the earth. The crystal air and laughing sun of October passed away, and November sank upon the shivering waste, chill and sombre as the tomb.

. . . .

At the middle of May, only eight men of the twenty-eight were alive, and of these half were suffering from disease.

This wintry purgatory wore away; the icy stalactites that hung from the cliffs fell crashing to the earth; the clamor of the wild geese was heard; the bluebirds appeared in the naked woods; the water-willows were covered with their soft caterpillar-like blossoms; the twigs of the swamp maple were flushed with ruddy bloom; the ash hung out its black-tufted flowers; the shadbush seemed a wreath of snow; the white stars of the bloodroot gleamed among the dank, fallen leaves; and in the young grass of the wet meadows, the marsh-marigolds shone like spots of gold.

Great was the joy of Champlain when he saw a sail-boat rounding the Point of Orleans, betokening that the spring had brought with it the longed-for succors.

From *Pioneers of France in the New World.*

1865

᚛

[W. E. Gladstone]

["His attack on the tree"]

The Liberals were returned to power with a majority of some 112 seats…. On 1 December, 1868, Gladstone was cutting down a tree in the park at Hawarden, when a telegram was delivered. It informed him that the Queen's secretary, General Grey, would arrive from Windsor that evening. "Very significant," was Gladstone's comment, as he took up the axe and resumed his attack on the tree. After a few minutes he ceased, and resting on the handle of the axe, he exclaimed to his guest, the Hon. Evelyn Ashley, a son of Lord Shaftesbury, in a voice of deep earnestness and with an intense expression: "My mission is to pacify Ireland." He then turned once more to the tree and said not another word until it was down.

………

[Gladstone] was 80 on 29 December, 1889, but he still cut down trees in his park at Hawarden, and presented chips to the hordes of admirers from all parts of the kingdom who flocked thither to stare at him. He laughed at Sir Andrew Clark who had been asked by Lord Granville and Lord Spencer to warn him that such violent exercise was very risky at his age, and that "something might snap at any moment." When he finally gave up tree-felling in October, 1890, he devoted many strenuous hours instead to rearranging the 28,000 books in his library.

Reprinted with the permission of John Murray (Publishers) Ltd.
From *Gladstone: A Biography*, by Philip Magnus, 1960.

1868

Thomas Henry Huxley
["The various kinds of living beings"]

What, truly, can seem to be more obviously different from one another, in faculty, in form, and in substance, than the various kinds of living beings? What community of faculty can there be between the bright-coloured lichen, which so nearly resembles a mere mineral incrustation of the bare rock on which it grows, and the painter, to whom it is instinct with beauty, or the botanist, whom it feeds with knowledge?

Again, think of the microscopic fungus – a mere infinitesmal ovoid particle, which finds space and duration enough to multiply into countless millions in the body of a living fly; and then of the wealth of foliage, the luxuriance of flower and fruit, which lies between this bald sketch of a plant and the giant pine of California, towering to the dimensions of a cathedral spire, or the Indian fig, which covers acres with its profound shadow, and endures while nations and empires come and go around its vast circumference.

From "On the Physical Basis of Life".

1868

Lewis Carroll

["The Cheshire Cat sitting on a bough of a tree"]

She was a little startled by seeing the Cheshire Cat sitting on a bough of a tree a few yards off.

This time it vanished quite slowly, beginning with the end of the tail, and ending with the grin, which remained some time after the rest of it had gone.

From *Alice's Adventures in Wonderland*. Drawings by John Tenniel.

1865

Thomas Hardy
["At the passing of the breeze"]

To dwellers in a wood almost every species of tree has its voice as well as its feature. At the passing of the breeze the fir-trees sob and moan no less distinctly than they rock; the holly whistles as it battles with itself; the ash hisses amid its quiverings; the beech rustles while its flat boughs rise and fall. And winter, which modifies the note of such trees as shed their leaves, does not destroy its individuality.

From *Under the Greenwood Tree,* I, by Thomas Hardy, London, Macmillan.

1872

Gerard Manley Hopkins
Binsey Poplars
felled 1879

My aspens dear, whose airy cages quelled,
Quelled or quenched in leaves the leaping sun,
All felled, felled, are all felled;
    Of a fresh and following folded rank
        Not spared, not one
        That dandled a sandalled
    Shadow that swam or sank
On meadow and river and wind-wandering weed-winding bank.

O if we but knew what we do
      When we delve or hew –
  Hack and rack the growing green!
      Since country is so tender
To touch, her being só slender,
That, like this sleek and seeing ball
But a prick will make no eye at all,
Where we, even where we mean
      To mend her we end her,
  When we hew or delve:
After-comers cannot guess the beauty been.
Ten or twelve, only ten or twelve
  Strokes of havoc únselve
      The sweet especial scene,
Rural scene, a rural scene,
Sweet especial rural scene.

———————

1879

✧

Sidney Lanier

A Ballad of Trees and the Master

Cf. Matt. XXVI: 36-46.

Into the woods my Master went,
Clean forspent, forspent.
Into the woods my Master came,
Forspent with love and shame.
But the olives they were not blind to Him,
The little gray leaves were kind to Him:
The thorn-tree had a mind to Him
When into the woods He came.

Out of the woods my Master went,
And He was well content.
Out of the woods my Master came,
Content with death and shame.
When Death and Shame would woo Him last,
From under the trees they drew Him last:
'Twas on a tree they slew Him – last
When out of the woods he came.

1880

Gerard Manley Hopkins

Spring and Fall:
to a young child

Márgarét, are you gríeving
Over Goldengrove unleaving?
Leáves, like the things of man, you
With your fresh thoughts care for, can you?
Áh! ás the heart grows older
It will come to such sights colder
By and by, nor spare a sigh
Though worlds of wanwood leafmeal lie;
And yet you wíll weep and know why.
Now no matter, child, the name:
Sórrow's spríngs áre the same.
Nor mouth had, no nor mind, expressed
What heart heard of, ghost guessed:
It ís the blight man was born for,
It is Margaret you mourn for.

1880

157

Richard Jefferies
Felling Trees

Much as I admired the timber about the Chace, I could not help sometimes wishing to have a chop at it. The pleasure of felling trees is never
lost. In youth, in manhood – so long as the arm can wield the axe – the
enjoyment is equally keen. As the heavy tool passes over the shoulder the
impetus of the swinging motion lightens the weight, and something like
a thrill passes through the sinews. Why is it so pleasant to strike? What
secret instinct is it that makes the delivery of a blow with axe or hammer
so exhilarating? The wilder frenzy of the sword – the fury of striking with
the keen blade, which overtakes men even now when they come hand to
hand, and which was once the life of battle – seems to arise from the same
feeling. Then, as the sharp edge of the axe cuts deep through the bark into
the wood, there is a second moment of gratification. The next blow sends
a chip spinning aside; and bye-the-bye never stand at the side of a
woodman, for a chip may score your cheek like a slash with a knife. But
the shortness of man's days will not allow him to cut down many trees. In
imagination I sometimes seem to hear the sounds of the axes that have
been ringing in the forests of America for a hundred years, and envy the
joy of the lumbermen as the tall pines toppled to the fall. Of our English
trees there is none so pleasant to chop as the lime; the steel enters into it
so easily.

In the enclosed portion of the park at Okebourne the boughs of the
trees descended and swept the sward. Nothing but sheep being permitted
to graze there, the trees grew in their natural form, the lower limbs
drooping downwards to the ground. Hedgerow timber is usually
'stripped' up at intervals, and the bushes, too, interfere with the expan-
sion of the branches; while the boughs of trees standing in the open fields
are nibbled off by cattle. But in that part of the park no cattle had fed in
the memory of man; so that the lower limbs, drooping by their own
weight, came arching to the turf. Each tree thus made a perfect bower.

The old woodmen who worked in the Chace told me it used to be said
that elm ought only to be thrown on two days of the year – *i.e.* the 31st of

December and the 1st of January. The meaning was that it should be cut in the very 'dead of the year,' when the sap had retired, so that the timber might last longer. The old folk took the greatest trouble to get their timber well seasoned, which is the reason why the woodwork in old houses has endured so well.

From *Round About a Great Estate.*

1880

𝒞

George Meredith
["Enter these enchanted woods"]

Enter these enchanted woods,
    You who dare.
Nothing harms beneath the leaves
More than waves a swimmer cleaves.
Toss your heart up with the lark,
Foot at peace with mouse and worm,
    Fair you fare.
Only at a dread of dark
Quaver, and they quit their form:
Thousand eyeballs under hoods
    Have you by the hair.
Enter these enchanted woods,
    You who dare.

Here the snake across your path
Stretches in his golden bath:
Mossy-footed squirrels leap
Soft as winnowing plumes of Sleep:
Yaffles on a chuckle skim
Low to laugh from branches dim:

Up the pine, where sits the star,
Rattles deep the moth-winged jar.
Each has business of his own;
But should you distrust a tone,
 Then beware.
Shudder all the haunted roods,
All the eyeballs under hoods
 Shroud you in their glare.
Enter these enchanted woods,
 You who dare.

From "The Woods of Westermain".

1883

James W. Wells
[The Brazilian forest]

It was very tedious work, for we could only make slow progress in these tangled woods; the men worked well, but huge trees obstructed the route, too big to cut down, and necessitating many a *détour*, every tree that was felled brought with it a mass of vines and interlaced foliage. There are very few flowers in the undergrowth of these woods; they only blossom high up above us or in the margins in the forests, where the sun can reach them, but there are numberless things of interest, variegated, coloured, and curious leaves, strangely shaped vines and parasites, orchids, huge buttressed trees, curious, pungent, or aromatic odours, the most usual being a strong peppery scent that appears to be common to many plants…. Insects alone afford a study, for there are beetles great and small, black beetles, green beetles, blue beetles, and spotted beetles; there is also a pretty butterfly with long, narrow, dark wings, tipped with vermilion, and as it flutters in the dark shade it appears like two fluttering, fiery eyes.

....

I have not seen the famed American backwoodsmen, but I do not think they can excel a skilled Brazilian *matutor* in general forest-clearing work; every stroke of billhook or axe is applied just where it should be, and it is rare that a slip occurs.... Ready, the axes fall with measured stroke and sure, hewing out wedge-like slices, every blow falls powerfully and unerringly, steadily given; they shout between the blows, anything that occurs to them, "*O! paú duro*" (Oh! hard wood!), etc., the speed increases, the blows fall quicker, a cleanly cut, wedge-like opening appears on each side, suddenly a startling crack is heard like the report of a pistol, the trunk slightly heels over, there is a rustle of foliage, a tightening of the interlacing vines; the axes are applied with increased energy, the chips fly about, again another report, a few more blows, a series of crackling reports, the stately trunk heels over, it falls with a rush amidst the shouts of the men, and bearing down a load of vines and bushes, crushing to the ground all small trees in its path, and there lies to rot, a splendid log of often valuable cabinet-wood.

....

Out in the open bush and scrub-land the sun's rays are powerful, but in the shade of these forests the air is damp and cool; in the sun one feels roasted and the skin browns and blisters, here one becomes steamed and blanched.

From *Exploring and Travelling Three Thousand Miles Through Brazil*, V.

1886

Thomas Hardy
["The ingress of the winter months"]

Although the time of bare boughs had now set in, there were sheltered hollows amid the Hintock plantations and copses in which a more tardy leave-taking than on windy summits was the rule with the foliage. This caused here and there an apparent mixture of the seasons; so that in some of the dells that they passed by holly-berries in full red were found growing beside oak and hazel whose leaves were as yet not far removed from green, and brambles whose verdure was rich and deep as in the month of August. To Grace these well-known peculiarities were as an old painting restored.

Now could be beheld that change from the handsome to the curious which the features of a wood undergo at the ingress of the winter months. Angles were taking the place of curves, and reticulations of surfaces – a change constituting a sudden lapse from the ornate to the primitive on Nature's canvas, and comparable to a retrogressive step from the art of an advanced school of painting to that of the Pacific Islander.

....

They went noiselessly over mats of starry moss, rustled through interspersed tracts of leaves, skirted trunks with spreading roots, whose mossed rinds made them like hands, wearing green gloves; elbowed old elms and ashes with great forks, in which stood pools of water that overflowed on rainy days, and ran down their stems in green cascades. On older trees still than these, huge lobes of fungi grew like lungs. Here, as everywhere, the Unfulfilled Intention, which makes life what it is, was as obvious as it could be among the depraved crowds of a city slum. The leaf was deformed, the curve was crippled, the taper was interrupted; the lichen ate the vigour of the stalk, and the ivy slowly strangled to death the promising sapling.

They dived amid beeches under which nothing grew, the younger boughs still retaining their hectic leaves, that rustled in the breeze with a sound almost metallic, like the sheet-iron foliage of the fabled Jarnvid wood. Some flecks of white in Grace's drapery had enabled Giles to keep her and her father in view till this time; but now he lost sight of them, and was obliged to follow by ear – no difficult matter, for on the line of their course every wood-pigeon rose from its perch with a continued clash, dashing its wings against the branches with wellnigh force enough to break every quill. By taking the track of this noise he soon came to a stile.

From *The Woodlanders*, VII, by Thomas Hardy, London, Macmillan.

1887

Archibald Lampman
In October

Along the waste, a great way off, the pines
  Like tall slim priests of storm, stand up and bar
The low long strip of dolorous red that lines
  The under west, where wet winds moan afar.
The cornfields all are brown, and brown the meadows
  With the blown leaves' wind-heapèd traceries,
And the brown thistle stems that cast no shadows,
  And bear no bloom for bees.

As slowly earthward leaf by red leaf slips,
  The sad trees rustle in chill misery,
A soft strange inner sound of pain-crazed lips,
  That move and murmur incoherently;
As if all leaves, that yet have breath, were sighing,
  With pale hushed throats, for death is at the door,
So many low soft masses for the dying
  Sweet leaves that live no more.

Here I will sit upon this naked stone,
  Draw my coat closer with my numbèd hands,
And hear the ferns sigh, and the wet woods moan,
  And send my heart out to the ashen lands;
And I will ask myself what golden madness,
  What balmèd breaths of dreamland spicery,
What visions of soft laughter and light sadness
  Were sweet last month to me.

The dry dead leaves flit by with thin weird tunes,
    Like failing murmurs of some conquered creed,
Graven in mystic markings with strange runes,
    That none but stars and biting winds may read;
Here I will wait a little; I am weary,
    Not torn with pain of any lurid hue,
But only still and very gray and dreary,
    Sweet sombre lands, like you.

1888

Sir James George Frazer

["A strange and recurring tragedy"]

Who does not know Turner's picture of the Golden Bough? The scene, suffused with the golden glow of imagination in which the divine mind of Turner steeped and transfigured even the fairest natural landscape, is a dream-like vision of the little woodland lake of Nemi – "Diana's Mirror," as it was called by the ancients. No one who has seen that calm water, lapped in a green hollow of the Alban hills, can ever forget it. The two characteristic Italian villages which slumber on its banks, and the equally Italian palace whose terraced gardens descend steeply to the lake, hardly break the stillness and even the solitariness of the scene. Diana herself might still linger by this lonely shore, still haunt these woodlands wild.

In antiquity this sylvan landscape was the scene of a strange and recurring tragedy. On the northern shore of the lake, right under the precipitous cliffs on which the modern village of Nemi is perched, stood the sacred grove and sanctuary of Diana Nemorensis, or Diana of the Wood. The lake and the grove were sometimes known as the lake and grove of Aricia. But the town of Aricia (the modern La Riccia) was situated about three miles off, at the foot of the Alban Mount, and separated by a steep descent from the lake, which lies in a small crater-like hollow on the mountain side. In this sacred grove there grew a certain tree round which

J. M. W. Turner, "The Golden Bough." Engraved by J. T. Willmore.
1856

at any time of the day, and probably far into the night, a grim figure might be seen to prowl. In his hand he carried a drawn sword, and he kept peering warily about him as if at every instant he expected to be set upon by an enemy. He was a priest and a murderer; and the man for whom he looked was sooner or later to murder him and hold the priesthood in his stead. Such was the rule of the sanctuary. A candidate for the priesthood could only succeed to office by slaying the priest, and having slain him, he retained office till he was himself slain by a stronger or a craftier.

From *The Golden Bough*, by Sir James George Frazer, London, Macmillan.

1890

Stephen Crane
[Sounds in the forest]

The trees began softly to sing a hymn of twilight. The sun sank until slanted bronze rays struck the forest. There was a lull in the noises of insects as if they had bowed their beaks and were making a devotional pause. There was silence save for the chanted chorus of the trees.

Then, upon this stillness, there suddenly broke a tremendous clangor of sounds. A crimson roar came from the distance.

The youth stopped. He was transfixed by this terrific medley of all noises. It was as if worlds were being rended. There was the ripping sound of musketry and the breaking crash of the artillery.

His mind flew in all directions. He conceived the two armies to be at each other panther fashion. He listened for a time. Then he began to run in the direction of the battle. He saw that it was an ironical thing for him to be running thus toward that which he had been at such pains to avoid. But he said, in substance, to himself that if the earth and the moon were about to clash, many persons would doubtless plan to get upon the roofs to witness the collision.

As he ran, he became aware that the forest had stopped its music, as if at last becoming capable of hearing the foreign sounds. The trees hushed and stood motionless. Everything seemed to be listening to the crackle and clatter and ear-shaking thunder. The chorus pealed over the still earth.

. . . .

He went rapidly on. He wished to come to the edge of the forest that he might peer out.

As he hastened, there passed through his mind pictures of stupendous conflicts. His accumulated thought upon such subjects was used to form scenes. The noise was as the voice of an eloquent being, describing.

Sometimes the brambles formed chains and tried to hold him back. Trees, confronting him, stretched out their arms and forbade him to pass. After its previous hostility this new resistance of the forest filled him with a fine bitterness. It seemed that Nature could not be quite ready to kill him.

But he obstinately took roundabout ways, and presently he was where he could see long gray walls of vapor where lay battle lines.

From *The Red Badge of Courage*, VIII.

1895

Thomas Hardy
In a Wood

Pale beech and pine so blue,
    Set in one clay,
Bough to bough cannot you
    Live out your day?
When the rains skim and skip,
Why mar sweet comradeship,
Blighting with poison-drip
    Neighbourly spray?

Heart-halt and spirit-lame,
　　City-opprest,
Unto this wood I came
　　As to a nest;
Dreaming that sylvan peace
Offered the harrowed ease –
Nature a soft release
　　From men's unrest.

But, having entered in,
　　Great growths and small
Show them to men akin –
　　Combatants all!
Sycamore shoulders oak,
Bines the slim sapling yoke,
Ivy-spun halters choke
　　Elms stout and tall.

Touches from ash, O wych,
　　Sting you like scorn!
You, too, brave hollies, twitch
　　Sidelong from thorn.
Even the rank poplars bear
Lothly a rival's air,
Cankering in black despair
　　If overborne.

Since, then, no grace I find
　　Taught me of trees,
Turn I back to my kind,
　　Worthy as these.
There at least smiles abound,
There discourse trills around,
There, now and then, are found
　　Life-loyalties.

From *The Woodlanders*, by Thomas Hardy, London, Macmillan.

1896

Aubrey Beardsley, "Merlin and Nimue." From Sir Thomas Malory's Le Morte Darthur.

1893-4

℘

A. E. Housman
["On Wenlock Edge"]

On Wenlock Edge the wood's in trouble;
   His forest fleece the Wrekin heaves;
The gale, it plies the saplings double,
   And thick on Severn snow the leaves.

'Twould blow like this through holt and hanger
   When Uricon the city stood:
'Tis the old wind in the old anger,
   But then it threshed another wood.

Then, 'twas before my time, the Roman
   At yonder heaving hill would stare:
The blood that warms an English yeoman,
   The thoughts that hurt him, they were there.

There, like the wind through woods in riot,
   Through him the gale of life blew high;
The tree of man was never quiet:
   Then 'twas the Roman, now 'tis I.

The gale, it plies the saplings double,
   It blows so hard, 'twill soon be gone:
To-day the Roman and his trouble
   Are ashes under Uricon.

––––––––––

From *A Shropshire Lad*, XXXI, by A. E. Housman, London,
Grant Richards Ltd.

1896

Thomas Hardy
The Ivy-Wife

I longed to love a full-boughed beech
    And be as high as he:
I stretched an arm within his reach,
    And signalled unity.
But with his drip he forced a breach
    And tried to poison me.

I gave the grasp of partnership
    To one of other race –
A plane: he barked him strip by strip
    From upper bough to base;
And me therewith; for gone my grip,
    My arms could not enlace.

In new affection next I strove
    To coll an ash I saw,
And he in trust received my love;
    Till with my soft green claw
I cramped and bound him as I wove...
    Such was my love: ha-ha!

By this I gained his strength and height
    Without his rivalry.
But in my triumph I lost sight
    Of afterhaps. Soon he,
Being bark-bound, flagged, snapped, fell outright,
    And in his fall felled me!

The Ivy-Wife, by Thomas Hardy, London, Macmillan.

1898

∾

Mark Twain
["At the farm"]

I spent some part of every year at the farm until I was twelve or thirteen years old. The life which I led there with my cousins was full of charm, and so is the memory of it yet. I can call back the solemn twilight and mystery of the deep woods, the earthy smells, the faint odors of the wild flowers, the sheen of rain-washed foliage, the rattling clatter of drops when the wind shook the trees, the far-off hammering of woodpeckers and the muffled drumming of wood pheasants in the remoteness of the forest, the snapshot glimpses of disturbed wild creatures scurrying through the grass – I can call it all back and make it as real as it ever was, and as blessed. I can call back the prairie, and its loneliness and peace, and a vast hawk hanging motionless in the sky, with his wings spread wide and the blue of the vault showing through the fringe of their end feathers. I can see the woods in their autumn dress, the oaks purple, the hickories washed with gold, the maples and the sumachs luminous with crimson fires, and I can hear the rustle made by the fallen leaves as we plowed through them. I can see the blue clusters of wild grapes hanging among the foliage of the saplings, and I remember the taste of them and the smell. I know how the wild blackberries looked and how they tasted; and the same with the paw paws, the hazelnuts, and the persimmons; and I can feel the thumping rain, upon my head, of hickory nuts and walnuts when we were out in the frosty dawn to scramble for them with the pigs, and the gusts of wind loosed them and sent them down. I know the stain of blackberries, and how pretty it is, and I know the stain of walnut hulls, and how little it minds soap and water, also what grudged experience it had of either of them. I know the taste of maple sap, and when to gather it, and how to arrange the troughs and the delivery tubes, and how to boil down the juice, and how to hook the sugar after it is made, also how much better hooked sugar tastes than any that is honestly come by, let bigots say what they will.

From "Early Days," *Mark Twain's Autobiography.*

1898

§

Charles G. D. Roberts
The Solitary Woodsman

When the grey lake-water rushes
Past the dripping alder-bushes,
   And the bodeful autumn wind
In the fir-tree weeps and hushes, –

When the air is sharply damp
Round the solitary camp,
   And the moose-bush in the thicket
Glimmers like a scarlet lamp, –

When the birches twinkle yellow,
And the cornel bunches mellow,
   And the owl across the twilight
Trumpets to his downy fellow, –

When the nut-fed chipmunks romp
Through the maples' crimson pomp,
   And the slim viburnum flushes
In the darkness of the swamp, –

When the blueberries are dead,
When the rowan clusters red,
   And the shy bear, summer-sleekened,
In the bracken makes his bed, –

On a day there comes once more
To the latched and lonely door,
   Down the wood-road striding silent,
One who has been here before.

Green spruce branches for his head,
Here he makes his simple bed,
    Couching with the sun, and rising
When the dawn is frosty red.

All day long he wanders wide
With the grey moss for his guide,
    And his lonely axe-stroke startles
The expectant forest-side.

Toward the quiet close of day
Back to camp he takes his way,
    And about his sober footsteps
Unafraid the squirrels play.

On his roof the red leaf falls,
At his door the bluejay calls,
    And he hears the wood-mice hurry
Up and down his rough log walls;

Hears the laughter of the loon
Thrill the dying afternoon;
    Hears the calling of the moose
Echo to the early moon.

And he hears the partridge drumming,
The belated hornet humming, –
    All the faint, prophetic sounds
That foretell the winter's coming.

And the wind about his eaves
Through the chilly night-wet grieves,
    And the earth's dumb patience fills him,
Fellow to the falling leaves.

From *New York Nocturnes, and Other Poems,* by Charles G. D. Roberts,
Lamson, Wolffe Publishers, Boston.

1898

Joseph Conrad

["Wanderers on a prehistoric earth"]

"Sometimes we came upon a station close by the bank, clinging to the skirts of the unknown, and the white men rushing out of a tumble-down hovel, with great gestures of joy and surprise and welcome, seemed very strange – had the appearance of being held there captive by a spell. The word 'ivory' would ring in the air for a while – and on we went again into the silence, along empty reaches, round the still bends, between the high walls of our winding way, reverberating in hollow claps the ponderous beat of the stern-wheel. Trees, trees, millions of trees, massive, immense, running up high; and at their foot, hugging the bank against the stream, crept the little begrimed steamboat, like a sluggish beetle crawling on the floor of a lofty portico. It made you feel very small, very lost, and yet it was not altogether depressing, that feeling. After all, if you were small, the grimy beetle crawled on – which was just what you wanted it to do. Where the pilgrims imagined it crawled to I don't know. To some place where they expected to get something, I bet! For me it crawled towards Kurtz – exclusively; but when the steam-pipes started leaking we crawled very slow. The reaches opened before us and closed behind, as if the forest had stepped leisurely across the water to bar the way for our return. We penetrated deeper and deeper into the heart of darkness. It was very quiet there. At night sometimes the roll of drums behind the curtain of trees would run up the river and remain sustained faintly, as if hovering in the air high over our heads, till the first break of day. Whether it meant war, peace, or prayer we could not tell. The dawns were heralded by the descent of a chill stillness; the woodcutters slept, their fires burned low; the snapping of a twig would make you start. We were wanderers on a prehistoric earth, on an earth that wore the aspect of an unknown planet. We could have fancied ourselves the first of men taking possession of an accursed inheritance, to be subdued at the cost of profound anguish and of excessive toil. But suddenly, as we struggled round a bend, there would be a glimpse of rush walls, of peaked grass-roofs, a burst of yells, a whirl of black limbs, a mass of hands clapping, of feet stamping, of bodies swaying, of eyes rolling, under the droop of heavy and motionless foliage. The steamer toiled along slowly on the edge of a black and incomprehensible frenzy. The prehistoric man was cursing us, praying to us, welcoming us – who could tell? We were cut off from the comprehension of our surroundings; we glided past like phantoms, wondering and secretly appalled, as sane men would be before an enthusiastic outbreak in a madhouse. We could not understand because we were too far and could not remember, because we were travelling in the night of first ages, of those ages that are gone, leaving hardly a sign – and no memories."

From "Heart of Darkness," II.

1899

⌒

Ralph Connor

["Indomitable faith and courage"]

From the farthest reaches of the Ottawa down the St. Lawrence to Quebec the Macdonald gang of Glengarry men was famous.... They were sons of the men who had come from the highlands and islands of Scotland in the early years of the last century. Driven from homes in the land of their fathers, they had set themselves with indomitable faith and courage to hew from the solid forest homes for themselves and their children that none might take from them. These pioneers were bound together by ties of blood, but also by bonds stronger than those of blood. Their loneliness, their triumphs, their sorrows, born of their common life-long conflict with the forest and its fierce beasts, knit them in bonds close and enduring. The sons born to them and reared in the heart of the pine forests grew up to witness that heroic struggle with stern nature and to take their part in it. And mighty men they were. Their life bred in them hardiness of frame, alertness of sense, readiness of resource, endurance, superb self-reliance, a courage that grew with peril, and withal a certain wildness which at times deepened into ferocity. By their fathers the forest was dreaded and hated, but the sons, with rifles in hand, trod its pathless stretches without fear, and with their broad-axes they took toll of their ancient foe. For while in spring and summer they farmed their narrow fields, and rescued new lands from the brûlé, in winter they sought the forest, and back on their own farms or in "the shanties" they cut saw-logs, or made square timber, their only source of wealth. The shanty life of the early fifties of last century was not the luxurious thing of today. It was full of privation, for the men were poorly housed and fed, and of peril, for the making of the timber and the getting it down the smaller rivers to the big water was a work of hardship and danger.

. . . .

Straight north from the St. Lawrence runs the road through the Indian Lands. At first its way lies through open country, from which the forest has been driven far back to the horizon on either side, for along the great river these many years villages have clustered, with open fields about them stretching far away. But when once the road leaves the Front, with its towns and villages and open fields, and passes beyond Martintown and over the North Branch, it reaches a country where the forest is more a feature of the landscape. And when some dozen or more of the cross-roads marking the concessions which lead off to east and west have been passed, the road seems to strike into a different world. The forest loses its conquered appearance, and dominates everything. There is forest every-where. It lines up close and thick along the road, and here and there quite overshadows it. It crowds in upon the little farms and shuts them off from one another and from the world outside, and peers in through the little windows of the log houses looking so small and lonely, but so beautiful in their forest frames. At the nineteenth crossroad the forest gives ground a little, for here the road runs right past the new brick church, which is almost finished, and which will be opened in a few weeks.

From *The Man from Glengarry*, I, III

1901

Rudyard Kipling

["'This is *my* country,' said the lama"]

'Who goes to the Hills goes to his mother.' They had crossed the Siwaliks and the half-tropical Doon, left Mussoorie behind them, and headed north along the narrow hill-roads. Day after day they struck deeper into the huddled mountains, and day after day Kim watched the lama return to a man's strength. Among the terraces of the Doon he had leaned on the boy's shoulder, ready to profit by wayside halts. Under the great ramp to Mussoorie he drew himself together as an old hunter faces a well-remembered bank, and where he should have sunk exhausted swung his long draperies about him, drew a deep double-lungful of the diamond air, and walked as only a hillman can. Kim, plains-bred and plains-fed, sweated and panted astonished. 'This is *my* country,' said the lama. 'Beside Such-zen, this is flatter than a rice-field'; and with steady, driving strokes from the loins he strode upwards. But it was on the steep downhill marches, three thousand feet in three hours, that he went utterly away from Kim, whose back ached with holding back, and whose big toe was nigh cut off by his grass sandal-string. Through the speckled shadow of the great deodar-forests; through oak feathered and plumed with ferns; birch, ilex, rhododendron, and pine, out on to the bare hill-sides' slippery sunburnt grass, and back into the woodlands' coolth again, till oak gave way to bamboo and palm of the valley, the lama swung untiring.

From *Kim*, XIII, by Rudyard Kipling, London, Macmillan.

1901

Ernest Thompson Seton
Sam's Woodcraft Exploit

Sam's "long suit," as he put it, was axemanship. He was remarkable even in this land of the axe, and, of course, among the "Injuns" he was a marvel. Yan might pound away for half an hour at some block that he was trying to split and make no headway, till Sam would say, "Yan, hit it right there," or perhaps take the axe and do it for him; then at one tap the block would fly apart. There was no rule for this happy hit. Sometimes it was above the binding knot, sometimes beside it, sometimes right in the middle of it, and sometimes in the end of the wood away from the binder altogether – often at the unlikeliest places. Sometimes it was done by a simple stroke, sometimes a glancing stroke, sometimes with the grain or again angling, and sometimes a compound of one or more of each kind of blow; but whatever was the right stroke, Sam seemed to know it instinctively and applied it to exactly the right spot, the only spot where the hard, tough log was open to attack, and rarely failed to make it tumble apart as though it were a trick got ready beforehand. He did not brag about it. He simply took it for granted that he was the master of the art, and as such the others accepted him.

On one occasion Yan, who began to think he now had some skill, was whacking away at a big, tough stick till he had tried, as he thought, every possible combination and still could make no sign of a crack. Then Guy insisted on "showing him how," without any better result.

"Here, Sam," cried Yan, "I'll bet this is a baffler for you."

Sam turned the stick over, selected a hopeless-looking spot, one as yet not touched by the axe, set the stick on end, poured a cup of water on the place, then, when that had soaked in, he struck with all his force a single straight blow at the line where the grain spread to embrace the knot. The aim was true to a hair and the block flew open.

"Hooray!" shouted Little Beaver in admiration.

"Pooh!" said Sapwood. "That was just chance. He couldn't do that again."

"Not to the same stick!" retorted Yan. He recognized the consummate skill and the cleverness of knowing that the cup of water was just what was needed to rob the wood of its spring and turn the balance.

But Guy continued contemptuously, "I had it started for him."

"*I* think that should count a *coup*," said Little Beaver.

"Coup nothin'," snorted the Third War Chief, in scorn. "I'll give you something to do that'll try if you can chop. Kin you chop a six-inch tree down in three minutes an' throw it up the wind?"

"What kind o' tree?" asked the Woodpecker.

"Oh, any kind."

"I'll bet you five dollars I kin cut down a six-inch White Pine in *two* minutes an' throw it any way I want to. You pick out the spot for me to lay it. Mark it with a stake an' I'll drive the stake."

"I don't think any of the Tribe has five dollars to bet. If you can do it we'll give you a *grand coup* feather," answered Little Beaver.

"No spring pole," said Guy, eager to make it impossible.

"All right," replied the Woodpecker; "I'll do it without using a spring pole."

So he whetted up his axe, tried the lower margin of the head, found it was a trifle out of the true – that is, its under curve centered, not on the handle one span down, but half an inch out from the handle. A nail driven into the point of the axe-eye corrected this and the chiefs went forth to select a tree. A White Pine that measured roughly six inches through was soon found, and Sam was allowed to clear away the brush around it. Yan and Guy now took a stout stake and, standing close to the tree, looked up the trunk. Of course, every tree in the woods leans one way or another, and it was easy to see that this leaned slightly southward. What wind there was came from the north, so Yan decided to set the stake due north.

Sam's little Japanese eyes twinkled. But Guy, who, of course, knew something of chopping, fairly exploded with scorn. "Pooh! What do you know? That's easy; any one can throw it straight up the wind. Give him a cornering shot and let him try. There, now," and Guy set the stake off to the northwest. "Now, smarty. Let's see you do that."

"All right. You'll see me. Just let me look at it a minute."

Sam walked round the tree, studied its lean and the force of the wind on its top, rolled up his sleeves, slipped his suspenders, spat on his palms, and, standing to west of the tree, said "*Ready.*"

Yan had his watch out and shouted "*Go.*"

Two firm, unhasty strokes up on the south side of the tree left a clean nick across and two inches deep in the middle. The chopper then stepped forward one pace and on the north-northwesterly side, eighteen inches lower down than the first cut, after reversing his hands – which is what few can do – he rapidly chopped a butt-kerf. Not a stroke was hasty; not a blow went wrong. The first chips that flew were ten inches long, but they quickly dwindled as the kerf sank in. The butt-kerf was two-thirds through the tree when Yan called "One minute up." Sam stopped work, apparently without cause, leaned one hand against the south side of the tree and gazed unconcernedly up at its top.

"Hurry up, Sam. You're losing time!" called his friend. Sam made no reply. He was watching the wind pushes and waiting for a strong one. It came – it struck the tree-top. There was an ominous crack, but Sam had left enough and pushed hard to make sure; as soon as the recoil began he struck in very rapid succession three heavy strokes, cutting away all the remaining wood on the west side and leaving only a three-inch triangle of uncut fibre. All the weight was now northwest of this. The tree toppled that way, but swung around on the uncut part; another puff of wind gave help, the swing was lost, the tree crashed down to the northwest and drove the stake right out of sight in the ground.

"Hooray! Hooray! Hooray! One minute and forty-five seconds!" How Yan did cheer. Sam was silent, but his eyes looked a little less dull and stupid than usual, and Guy said "Pooh! That's nothin'."

Yan took out his pocket rule and went to the stump. As soon as he laid it on, he exclaimed "Seven and one-half inches through where you cut," and again he had to swing his hat and cheer.

"Well, old man, you surely did it that time. That's a grand coup if ever I saw one," and so, notwithstanding Guy's proposal to "leave it to Caleb," Sam got his grand Eagle feather as Axeman A I of the Sanger Indians.

From *Two Little Savages*, by Ernest Thompson Seton, New York, Doubleday Page.

1903

◔◕

W. H. Hudson

["That leafy cloudland"]

I spent several hours in this wild paradise, which was so much more delightful than the extensive gloomier forests I had so often penetrated in Guayana: for here, if the trees did not attain to such majestic proportions, the variety of vegetable forms was even greater; as far as I went it was nowhere dark under the trees, and the number of lovely parasites everywhere illustrated the kindly influence of light and air. Even where the trees were largest the sunshine penetrated, subdued by the foliage to exquisite greenish-golden tints, filling the wide lower spaces with tender half-lights, and faint blue-and-grey shadows. Lying on my back and gazing up, I felt reluctant to rise and renew my ramble. For what a roof was that above my head! Roof I call it, just as the poets in their poverty sometimes describe the infinite ethereal sky by that word; but it was no more roof-like and hindering to the soaring spirit than the higher clouds that float in changing forms and tints, and like the foliage chasten the intolerable noonday beams. How far above me seemed that leafy cloudland into which I gazed! Nature, we know, first taught the architect to produce by long colonnades the illusion of distance; but the light-excluding roof prevents him from getting the same effect above. Here Nature is unapproachable with her green, airy canopy, a sun-impregnated cloud – cloud above cloud; and though the highest may be unreached by the eye, the beams yet filter through, illuming the wide spaces beneath – chamber succeeded by chamber, each with its own special lights and shadows. Far above me, but not nearly so far as it seemed, the tender gloom of one such chamber or space is traversed now by a golden shaft of light falling through some break in the upper foliage, giving a strange glory to everything it touches – projecting leaves, and beard-like tuft of moss, and snaky bush-rope. And in the most open part of that most open space, suspended on nothing to the eye, the shaft reveals a tangle of shining silver threads – the web of some large tree-spider. These seemingly distant, yet distinctly visible threads, serve to remind me that the human artist is only able to get his horizontal distance by a monotonous reduplication of pillar and arch, placed at regular intervals, and that the least departure from this order would destroy the effect. But Nature produces her effects at random, and seems only to increase the beautiful illusion by that infinite variety of decoration in which she revels, binding tree to tree in a tangle of anaconda-like lianas, and dwindling down from these huge cables to airy webs and hair-like fibres that vibrate to the wind of the passing insect's wings.

From *Green Mansions*, II.

1904

Henry James
["A place prepared for high uses"]

The old informal earthy coach-road was a firm highway, wide and white – and ground to dust, for all its firmness, by the whirling motor; without which I might have followed it, back and back a little, into the near, into the far, country of youth – left lying, however, as the case stood, beyond the crest of the hill. Only the high rock-walls of the Ledges, the striking sign of the spot, were there; grey and perpendicular, with their lodged patches of shrub-like forest growth, and the immense floor, below them, where the Saco spreads and turns and the elms of the great general meadow stand about like candelabra (with their arms reversed) interspaced on a green table. There hung over these things the insistent hush of a September Sunday morning; nowhere greater than in the tended woods enclosing the admirable country home that I was able to enjoy as a centre for contemplation; woods with their dignity maintained by a large and artful clearance of undergrowth, and repaying this attention, as always, by something of the semblance of a sacred grove, a place prepared for high uses, even if for none rarer than high talk. There was a latent poetry – old echoes, ever so faint, that *would* come back; it made a general meaning, lighted the way to the great modern farm, all so contemporary and exemplary, so replete with beauty of beasts and convenience of man, with a positive dilettantism of care, but making one perhaps regret a little the big, dusky, heterogeneous barns, the more Bohemian bucolics, of the earlier time.

From *The American Scene*, I, iii.

1907

John Kendrick Bangs
The Pine

Let others have the maple trees,
 With all their garnered sweets.
Let others choose the mysteries
 Of leafy oak retreats.
I'll give to other men the fruit
 Of cherry and the vine.
Their claims to all I'll not dispute
 If I can have the pine.

I love it for its tapering grace,
 Its uplift straight and true.
I love it for the fairy lace
 It throws against the blue.
I love it for its quiet strength,
 Its hints of dreamy rest
As, stretching forth my weary length,
 I lie here as its guest.

The Pine
From Scribner's Magazine, *Jan.-June 1908*

No Persian rug for priceless fee
    Was e'er so richly made
As that the pine hath spread for me
    To woo me to its shade.
No kindly friend hath ever kept
    More faithful vigil by
A tired comrade as he slept
    Beneath his watchful eye.

But best of all I love it for
    Its soft, eternal green;
Through all the winter winds that roar
    It ever blooms serene,
And strengthens souls oppressed by fears,
    By troubles multiform,
To turn, amid the stress of tears,
    A smiling face to storm.

From *Scribner's Magazine.*
Jan.-June 1908

Kenneth Grahame
["The Wild Wood"]

"I see you don't understand, and I must explain it to you. Well, very long ago, on the spot where the Wild Wood waves now, before ever it had planted itself and grown up to what it now is, there was a city – a city of people, you know. Here, where we are standing, they lived, and walked, and talked, and slept, and carried on their business. Here they stabled their horses and feasted, from here they rode out to fight or drove out to trade. They were a powerful people, and rich, and great builders. They built to last, for they thought their city would last for ever."

"But what has become of them all?" asked the Mole.

"Who can tell?" said the Badger. "People come – they stay for a while, they flourish, they build – and they go. It is their way. But we remain. There were badgers here, I've been told, long before that same city ever came to be. And now there are badgers here again. We are an enduring lot, and we may move out for a time, but we wait, and are patient, and back we come. And so it will ever be."

"Well, and when they went at last, those people?" said the Mole.

"When they went," continued the Badger, "the strong winds and persistent rains took the matter in hand, patiently, ceaselessly, year after year. Perhaps we badgers too, in our small way, helped a little – who knows? It was all down, down, down, gradually – ruin and levelling and disappearance. Then it was all up, up, up, gradually, as seeds grew to saplings, and saplings to forest trees, and bramble and fern came creeping in to help. Leaf-mould rose and obliterated, streams in their winter freshets brought sand and soil to clog and to cover, and in course of time our home was ready for us again, and we moved in. Up above us, on the surface, the same thing happened. Animals arrived, liked the look of the place, took up their quarters, settled down, spread, and flourished. They didn't bother themselves about the past – they never do; they're too busy. The place was a bit humpy and hillocky, naturally, and full of holes; but that was rather an advantage. And they don't bother about the future, either – the future when perhaps the people will move in again – for a time – as may very well be. The Wild Wood is pretty well populated by now; with all the usual lot, good, bad, and indifferent – I name no names. It takes all sorts to make a world. But I fancy you know something about them yourself by this time."

"I do indeed," said the Mole, with a slight shiver.

"Well, well," said the Badger, patting him on the shoulder, "it was your first experience of them, you see. They're not so bad really; and we must all live and let live. But I'll pass the word around to-morrow, and I think you'll have no further trouble. Any friend of *mine* walks where he likes in this country, or I'll know the reason why!"

From *The Wind in the Willows*, IV, by Kenneth Grahame, London, Methuen.

1908

Kenneth Grahame

[Mole and Rat encounter the great Pan]

A wide half-circle of foam and glinting lights and shining shoulders of green water, the great weir closed the backwater from bank to bank, troubled all the quiet surface with twirling eddies and floating foam-streaks, and deadened all other sounds with its solemn and soothing rumble. In midmost of the stream, embraced in the weir's shimmering arm-spread, a small island lay anchored, fringed close with willow and silver birch and alder. Reserved, shy, but full of significance, it hid whatever it might hold behind a veil, keeping it till the hour should come, and, with the hour, those who were called and chosen.

Slowly, but with no doubt or hesitation whatever, and in something of a solemn expectancy, the two animals passed through the broken tumultuous water and moored their boat at the flowery margin of the island. In silence they landed, and pushed through the blossom and scented herbage and undergrowth that led up to the level ground, till they stood on a little lawn of a marvellous green, set round with Nature's own orchard-trees – crab-apple, wild cherry, and sloe.

'This is the place of my song-dream, the place the music played to me,' whispered the Rat, as if in a trance. 'Here, in this holy place, here if anywhere, surely we shall find Him!'

Then suddenly the Mole felt a great Awe fall upon him, an awe that turned his muscles to water, bowed his head, and rooted his feet to the ground. It was no panic terror – indeed he felt wonderfully at peace and happy – but it was an awe that smote and held him and, without seeing, he knew it could only mean that some august Presence was very, very near. With difficulty he turned to look for his friend, and saw him at his side cowed, stricken, and trembling violently. And still there was utter silence in the populous bird-haunted branches around them; and still the light grew and grew.

Perhaps he would never have dared to raise his eyes, but that, though the piping was now hushed, the call and the summons seemed still dominant and imperious. He might not refuse, were Death himself waiting to strike him instantly, once he had looked with mortal eye on things rightly kept hidden. Trembling he obeyed, and raised his humble head; and then, in that utter clearness of the imminent dawn, while Nature, flushed with fulness of incredible colour, seemed to hold her breath for the event, he looked in the very eyes of the Friend and Helper; saw the backward sweep of the curved horns, gleaming in the growing daylight; saw the stern, hooked nose between the kindly eyes that were looking down on them humorously, while the bearded mouth broke into a half-smile at the corners; saw the rippling muscles on the arm that lay across the broad chest, the long supple hand still holding the pan-pipes only just fallen away from the parted lips; saw the splendid curves of the shaggy limbs disposed in majestic ease on the sward; saw, last of all, nestling between his very hooves, sleeping soundly in entire peace and contentment, the little, round, podgy, childish form of the baby otter. All this he saw, for one moment breathless and intense, vivid on the morning sky; and still, as he looked, he lived; and still, as he lived, he wondered.

'Rat!' he found breath to whisper, shaking. 'Are you afraid?'

'Afraid?' murmured the Rat, his eyes shining with unutterable love. 'Afraid! Of *Him*? O, never, never! And yet – and yet – O, Mole, I am afraid!'

Then the two animals, crouching to the earth, bowed their heads and did worship.

––––––––––

From *The Wind in the Willows*, VII, by Kenneth Grahame, London, Methuen.

1908

∾

Winston S. Churchill
["The forests of Uganda"]

For a whole day we crept through the skirts of the Hoima forest, amid an exuberance of vegetation which is scarcely describable. I had travelled through tropical forests in Cuba and India, and had often before admired their enchanting, yet sinister, luxuriance. But the forests of Uganda, for magnificence, for variety of form and colour, for profusion of brilliant life – plant, bird, insect, reptile, beast – for the vast scale and awful fecundity of the natural processes that are beheld at work, eclipsed, and indeed effaced, all previous impressions. One becomes, not without a secret sense of aversion, the spectator of an intense convulsion of life and death. Reproduction and decay are locked struggling in infinite embraces. In this glittering Equatorial slum huge trees jostle one another for room to live; slender growths stretch upwards – as it seems in agony – towards sunlight and life. The soil bursts with irrepressible vegetations. Every victor, trampling on the rotting mould of exterminated antagonists, soars aloft only to encounter another host of aerial rivals, to be burdened with masses of parasitic foliage, smothered in the glorious blossoms of creepers, laced and bound and interwoven with interminable tangles of vines and trailers. Birds are as bright as butterflies; butterflies are as big as birds. The air hums with flying creatures; the earth crawls beneath your foot. The telegraph-wire runs northward to Gondokoro through this vegetable labyrinth. Even its poles had broken into bud!

From *My African Journey,* by Winston S. Churchill, London, Hodder and Stoughton. Reproduced with permission of Curtis Brown Ltd., London, on behalf of The Estate of Sir Winston S. Churchill. Copyright Winston S. Churchill.

1908

"On the Don River," by Tom Thomson. Private collection. Published in
Tom Thomson: The Silence and the Storm, *by Harold Town and*
David Silcox, Toronto, McClelland and Stewart, 1977.

Reproduced with the permission of David Silcox.

ca. 1908

Thomas Hardy
The Pine Planters

(Marty South's Reverie)

I

We work here together
   In blast and breeze;
He fills the earth in,
   I hold the trees.

He does not notice
   That what I do
Keeps me from moving
   And chills me through.

He has seen one fairer
   I feel by his eye,
Which skims me as though
   I were not by.

And since she passed here
   He scarce has known
But that the woodland
   Holds him alone.

I have worked here with him
   Since morning shine,
He busy with his thoughts
   And I with mine.

I have helped him so many,
   So many days,
But never win any
   Small word of praise!

Shall I not sigh to him
   That I work on
Glad to be nigh to him
   Though hope is gone?

Nay, though he never
   Knew love like mine,
I'll bear it ever
   And make no sign!

II

From the bundle at hand here
   I take each tree,
And set it to stand, here
   Always to be;
When, in a second
   As if from fear
Of Life unreckoned
   Beginning here,
It starts a sighing
   Through day and night,
Though while there lying
   'Twas voiceless quite.

It will sigh in the morning,
   Will sigh at noon,
At the winter's warning,
   In wafts of June;
Grieving that never
   Kind Fate decreed
It should for ever
   Remain a seed,
And shun the welter
   Of things without,
Unneeding shelter
   From storm and drought.

Thus, all unknowing
   For whom or what
We set it growing
   In this bleak spot,
It still will grieve here
   Throughout its time,
Unable to leave here,
   Or change its clime:
Or tell the story
   Of us to-day
When, halt and hoary,
   We pass away.

The Pine Planters (Marty South's Reverie), by Thomas Hardy, London,
Macmillan.

1909

"Saki" (H. H. Munro)

["The worship of Pan never has died out"]

There was a sombre almost savage wildness about Yessney that was
certainly not likely to appeal to town-bred tastes, and Sylvia, notwithstanding her name, was accustomed to nothing much more sylvan than
"leafy Kensington." She looked on the country as something excellent and
wholesome in its way, which was apt to become troublesome if you encouraged it overmuch. Distrust of town-life had been a new thing with
her, born of her marriage with Mortimer, and she had watched with sat-
isfaction the gradual fading of what she called "the Jermyn-Street-look"
in his eyes as the woods and heather of Yessney had closed in on them
yesternight. Her will-power and strategy had prevailed; Mortimer would
stay.

Outside the morning-room windows was a triangular slope of turf,
which the indulgent might call a lawn, and beyond its low hedge of

neglected fuchsia bushes a steeper slope of heather and bracken dropped down into cavernous combes overgrown with oak and yew. In its wild open savagery there seemed a stealthy linking of the joy of life with the terror of unseen things. Sylvia smiled complacently as she gazed with a School-of-Art appreciation at the landscape, and then of a sudden she almost shuddered.

"It is very wild," she said to Mortimer, who had joined her; "one could almost think that in such a place the worship of Pan had never quite died out."

"The worship of Pan never has died out," said Mortimer. "Other newer gods have drawn aside his votaries from time to time, but he is the Nature-God to whom all must come back at last. He has been called the Father of all the Gods, but most of his children have been stillborn."

. . . .

Of Mortimer she saw very little; farm and woods and trout-streams seemed to swallow him up from dawn till dusk. Once, following the direction she had seen him take in the morning, she came to an open space in a nut copse, further shut in by huge yew trees, in the centre of which stood a stone pedestal surmounted by a small bronze figure of a youthful Pan. It was a beautiful piece of workmanship, but her attention was chiefly held by the fact that a newly cut bunch of grapes had been placed as an offering at its feet. Grapes were none too plentiful at the manor house, and Sylvia snatched the bunch angrily from the pedestal. Contemptuous annoyance dominated her thoughts as she strolled slowly homeward, and then gave way to a sharp feeling of something that was very near fright; across a thick tangle of undergrowth a boy's face was scowling at her, brown and beautiful, with unutterably evil eyes. It was a lonely pathway, all pathways round Yessney were lonely for the matter of that, and she sped forward without waiting to give a closer scrutiny to this sudden apparition. It was not till she had reached the house that she discovered that she had dropped the bunch of grapes in her flight.

"I saw a youth in the wood today," she told Mortimer that evening, "brown-faced and rather handsome, but a scoundrel to look at. A gipsy lad, I suppose."

"A reasonable theory," said Mortimer, "only there aren't any gipsies in these parts at present."

"Then who was he?" asked Sylvia, and as Mortimer appeared to have no theory of his own, she passed on to recount her finding of the votive offering.

"I suppose it was your doing," she observed: "it's a harmless piece of lunacy, but people would think you dreadfully silly if they knew of it."

"Did you meddle with it in any way?" asked Mortimer.

"I – I threw the grapes away. It seemed so silly," said Sylvia, watching Mortimer's impassive face for a sign of annoyance.

"I don't think you were wise to do that," he said reflectively. "I've heard it said that the Wood Gods are rather horrible to those who molest them."

"Horrible perhaps to those that believe in them, but you see I don't," retorted Sylvia.

"All the same," said Mortimer in his even, dispassionate tone, "I should avoid the woods and orchards if I were you and give a wide berth to the horned beasts on the farm."

It was all nonsense, of course, but in that lonely wood-girt spot nonsense seemed able to rear a bastard brood of uneasiness.

"Mortimer," said Sylvia suddenly, "I think we will go back to Town some time soon."

Her victory had not been so complete as she had supposed; it had carried her on to ground that she was already anxious to quit.

"I don't think you will ever go back to Town," said Mortimer.

From "The Music on the Hill," *Chronicles of Clovis*.

1911

~

Joyce Kilmer
Trees

I think that I shall never see
A poem lovely as a tree,

A tree whose hungry mouth is prest
Against the earth's sweet flowing breast;

A tree that looks to God all day,
And lifts her leafy arms to pray;

A tree that may in summer wear
A nest of robins in her hair;

Upon whose bosom snow has lain;
Who intimately lives with rain.

Poems are made by fools like me,
But only God can make a tree.

1913

~

Ogden Nash
Song of the Open Road

I think that I shall never see
A billboard lovely as a tree.
Indeed, unless the billboards fall
I'll never see a tree at all.

From *Verses From 1929 On* by Ogden Nash. Copyright 1932 by Ogden Nash. First appeared in *The New Yorker*. By permission of Little, Brown and Company.

ca. 1932

Robert Frost
Birches

When I see birches bend to left and right
Across the lines of straighter darker trees,
I like to think some boy's been swinging them.
But swinging doesn't bend them down to stay
As ice storms do. Often you must have seen them
Loaded with ice a sunny winter morning
After a rain. They click upon themselves
As the breeze rises, and turn many-colored
As the stir cracks and crazes their enamel.
Soon the sun's warmth makes them shed crystal shells
Shattering and avalanching on the snow crust –
Such heaps of broken glass to sweep away
You'd think the inner dome of heaven had fallen.
They are dragged to the withered bracken by the load,
And they seem not to break; though once they are bowed
So low for long, they never right themselves:
You may see their trunks arching in the woods
Years afterwards, trailing their leaves on the ground
Like girls on hands and knees that throw their hair
Before them over their heads to dry in the sun.
But I was going to say when Truth broke in
With all her matter of fact about the ice storm,
I should prefer to have some boy bend them
As he went out and in to fetch the cows –
Some boy too far from town to learn baseball,
Whose only play was what he found himself,
Summer or winter, and could play alone.
One by one he subdued his father's trees
By riding them down over and over again
Until he took the stiffness out of them,
And not one but hung limp, not one was left

For him to conquer. He learned all there was
To learn about not launching out too soon
And so not carrying the tree away
Clear to the ground. He always kept his poise
To the top branches, climbing carefully
With the same pains you use to fill a cup
Up to the brim, and even above the brim.
Then he flung outward, feet first, with a swish,
Kicking his way down through the air to the ground.
So was I once myself a swinger of birches.
And so I dream of going back to be.
It's when I'm weary of considerations,
And life is too much like a pathless wood
Where your face burns and tickles with the cobwebs
Broken across it, and one eye is weeping
From a twig's having lashed across it open.
I'd like to get away from earth awhile
And then come back to it and begin over.
May no fate willfully misunderstand me
And half grant what I wish and snatch me away
Not to return. Earth's the right place for love:
I don't know where it's likely to go better.
I'd like to go by climbing a birch tree,
And climb black branches up a snow-white trunk
Toward heaven, till the tree could bear no more,
But dipped its top and set me down again.
That would be good both going and coming back.
One could do worse than be a swinger of birches.

From *The Poetry of Robert Frost*, edited by Edward Connery Lathem,
© 1949 by Henry Holt & Co., Inc.

1914

✦

Louis Hémon
["The life of the woods"]

The icy road held alongside the frozen river. The houses on the other shore, each surrounded with its patch of cleared land, were sadly distant from one another. Behind the clearings, and on either side of them to the river's bank, it was always forest: a dark green background of cypress against which a lonely birch tree stood out here and there, its bole naked and white as the column of a ruined temple.

On the other side of the road the strip of cleared land was continuous and broader; the houses, set closer together, seemed an outpost of the village; but ever behind the bare fields marched the forest, following like a shadow, a gloomy frieze without end between white ground and grey sky.

....

After a couple of miles the road climbed a steep hill and entered the unbroken woods. The houses standing at intervals in the flat country all the way from the village came abruptly to an end, and there was no longer anything for the eye to rest upon but a wilderness of bare trunks rising out of the universal whiteness. Even the incessant dark green of balsam, spruce and grey pine was rare; the few young and living trees were lost among the endless dead, either lying on the ground and buried in snow, or still erect but stripped and blackened. Twenty years before great forest fires had swept through, and the new growth was only pushing its way amid the standing skeletons and the charred down-timber. Little hills followed one upon the other, and the road was a succession of ups and downs scarcely more considerable than the slopes of an ocean swell, from trough to crest, from crest to trough.

Maria Chapdelaine drew the cloak about her, slipped her hands under the warm robe of grey goat-skin and half closed her eyes. There was nothing to look at; in the settlements new houses and barns might go up from year to year, or be deserted and tumble into ruin; but the life of the woods is so unhurried that one must needs have more than the patience of a human being to await and mark its advance.

From *Maria Chapdelaine*, I, translated by W. H. Blake, 1921.

1914

Thomas Hardy

At Day-Close in November

The ten hours' light is abating,
    And a late bird wings across,
Where the pines, like waltzers waiting,
    Give their black heads a toss.

Beech leaves, that yellow the noon-time,
    Float past like specks in the eye;
I set every tree in my June time,
    And now they obscure the sky.

And the children who ramble through here
    Conceive that there never has been
A time when no tall trees grew here,
    That none will in time be seen.

At Day-Close in November, by Thomas Hardy, London, Macmillan.

1914

Edward Thomas

Lights Out

I have come to the borders of sleep,
The unfathomable deep
Forest, where all must lose
Their way, however straight
Or winding, soon or late:
They can not choose.

Many a road and track
That since the dawn's first crack
Up to the forest brink
Deceived the travellers,
Suddenly now blurs,
And in they sink.

Here love ends –
Despair, ambition ends;
All pleasure and all trouble,
Although most sweet or bitter,
Here ends, in sleep that is sweeter
Than tasks most noble.

There is not any book
Or face of dearest look
That I would not turn from now
To go into the unknown
I must enter, and leave, alone,
I know not how.

The tall forest towers:
Its cloudy foliage lowers
Ahead, shelf above shelf:
Its silence I hear and obey
That I may lose my way
And myself.

1916

$\sim$

Virginia Woolf
[Thinking about a Tree]

Wood is a pleasant thing to think about. It comes from a tree; and trees grow, and we don't know how they grow. For years and years they grow, without paying any attention to us, in meadows, in forests, and by the side of rivers – all things one likes to think about. The cows swish their tails beneath them on hot afternoons; they paint rivers so green that when a moorhen dives one expects to see its feathers all green when it comes up again. I like to think of the fish balanced against the stream like flags blown out; and of water-beetles slowly raising domes of mud upon the bed of the river. I like to think of the tree itself; first the close dry sensation of being wood; then the grinding of the storm; then the slow, delicious ooze of sap. I like to think of it, too, on winter's nights standing in the empty field with all leaves close-furled, nothing tender exposed to the iron bullets of the moon, a naked mast upon an earth that goes tumbling, tumbling, all night long. The song of birds must sound very loud and strange in June; and how cold the feet of insects must feel upon it, as they make laborious progresses up the creases of the bark, or sun themselves upon the thin green awning of the leaves, and look straight in front of them with diamond-cut red eyes…. One by one the fibres snap beneath the immense cold pressure of the earth, then the last storm comes and, falling, the highest branches drive deep into the ground again. Even so, life isn't done with; there are a million patient, watchful lives still for a tree, all over the world, in bedrooms, in ships, on the pavement, lining rooms, where men and women sit after tea, smoking cigarettes. It is full of peaceful thoughts, happy thoughts, this tree.

Excerpt from "The Mark on the Wall" in *A Haunted House and Other Short Stories* by Virginia Woolf, copyright © 1944 and renewed 1972 by Harcourt Brace & Company, reprinted by permission of the publisher.

1917

Siegfried Sassoon
["As long as there are some trees left standing upright"]

The pine-trees stood up dark and peaceful, looming against the pale sky where the moon was hid by clouds. The rain (that Sorley loved) was dripping quietly down, and there was the endless murmur of the wood like surf miles away. And the guns still rumbling at their damned bombardment. There's a line of beeches by the path to the camp. They are silent, they've no night music like the pines. They are waiting to sing their April lyric of young leaves. Waiting to dress themselves in their glory of green and luminous yellow. Trees are friendly things.

And I am very lucky to be able to find happiness so quickly. A few hundred yards and I am alone with the trees and the rain. So all is well. It is my evening prayer. And the war is of no importance as long as there are some trees left standing upright, with a clean wind to shake their branches. Beside these things, how grotesque and dull and licentious human nature appears. That mysterious life of growing things doesn't seem to have any significance for it. A few slang phrases, war-shop, a woman, a plate of food, a glass of beer and a smoke, is that really all? I can't believe it.

Reprinted with the permission of Faber and Faber Limited from *Siegfried Sassoon Diaries 1915-1918*, edited by Rupert Hart-Davis, London, 1983.

6 March 1917

Wilfred Owen
Miners

There was a whispering in my hearth,
    A sigh of the coal,
Grown wistful of a former earth
    It might recall.

"A shell-torn and well strafed wood in the Ypres Salient. Broodseinde Ridge.
4 November 1917." Ref. E(AUS).1147.

Reproduced with the permission of The Trustees of
The Imperial War Museum, London.

1917

I listened for a tale of leaves
    And smothered ferns;
Frond-forests; and the low, sly lives
    Before the fawns.

My fire might show steam-phantoms simmer
    From Time's old cauldron,
Before the birds made nests in summer,
    Or men had children.

But the coals were murmuring of their mine,
    And moans down there
Of boys that slept wry sleep, and men
    Writhing for air.

And I saw white bones in the cinder-shard.
    Bones without number;
For many hearts with coal are charred
    And few remember.

I thought of some who worked dark pits
    Of war, and died
Digging the rock where Death reputes
    Peace lies indeed.

Comforted years will sit soft-chaired
    In rooms of amber;
The years will stretch their hands, well-cheered
    By our lives' ember.

The centuries will burn rich loads
    With which we groaned,
Whose warmth shall lull their dreaming lids
    While songs are crooned.
But they will not dream of us poor lads
    Lost in the ground.

1918

☾

W. B. Yeats

["O may she live like some green laurel"]

May she become a flourishing hidden tree
That all her thoughts may like the linnet be,
And have no business but dispensing round
Their magnanimities of sound,
Nor but in merriment begin a chase,
Nor but in merriment a quarrel.
O may she live like some green laurel
Rooted in one dear perpetual place.

. . . .

And may her bridegroom bring her to a house
Where all's accustomed, ceremonious;
For arrogance and hatred are the wares
Peddled in the thoroughfares.
How but in custom and in ceremony
Are innocence and beauty born?
Ceremony's a name for the rich horn,
And custom for the spreading laurel tree.

———————

From "A Prayer for my Daughter."

———————

Reprinted with the permission of Simon & Schuster from *The Poems of W. B. Yeats: A New Edition*, edited by Richard J. Finneran. Copyright 1924 by Macmillan Publishing Company, renewed 1952 by Bertha Georgie Yeats.

1919

James Merrill
Paul Valéry: Palme

Veiling, barely, his dread
Beauty and its blaze,
An angel sets warm bread
And cool milk at my place.
His eyelids make the sign
Of prayer; I lower mine,
Words interleaving vision:
– Calm, calm, be ever calm!
Feel the whole weight a palm
Bears upright in profusion.

However its boughs yield
Beneath abundance, it
Is formally fulfilled
In bondage to thick fruit.
Wonder and see it grow!
One fiber, vibrant, slow,
Cleaving the hour fanwise,
Becomes a golden rule
To tell apart earth's pull
From heaven's gravities.

Svelte arbiter between
The shadow and the sun,
It takes much sibylline
Somnolent wisdom on.
Unstintingly to suffer
Hails and farewells, forever
Standing where it must stand…
How noble and how tender,
How worthy of surrender
To none but a god's hand!

The lightest gold-leaf murmur
Rings at a flick of air,
Invests with silken armor
The very desert. Here
This tree's undying voice
Upraised in the wind's hiss,
As fine sand sprays and stings,
To its own self is oracle
Complacent of the miracle
Whereby misfortune sings.

Held in an artless dream
Between blue sky and dune,
Secreting, dram by dram,
The honey of each noon,
What is this delectation
If not divine duration
That, without keeping time,
Can alter it, seduce
Into a steady juice
Love's volatile perfume?

At moments one despairs.
Should the adored duress
Ordain, despite your tears,
A spell of fruitlessness,
Do not call Wisdom cold
Who readies so much gold,
So much authority:
Rising in solemn pith
A green, eternal myth
Reaches maturity.

These days which, like yourself,
Seem empty and effaced
Have avid roots that delve
To work deep in the waste.
Their shaggy systems, fed
Where shade confers with shade,
Can never cease or tire,
At the world's heart are found
Still tracking that profound
Water the heights require.

Patience and still patience,
Patience beneath the blue!
Each atom of the silence
Knows what it ripens to.
The happy shock will come:
A dove alighting, some
Gentlest nudge, the breeze,
A woman's touch – before
You know it, the downpour
Has brought you to your knees!

Let populations be
Crumbled underfoot –
Palm, irresistibly –
Among celestial fruit!
Those hours were not in vain
So long as you retain
A lightness once they're lost;
Like one who, thinking, spends
His inmost dividends
To grow at any cost.

Translated by James Merrill. *Late Settings; Poems by James Merrill,*
Atheneum, New York, 1985. Used by permission of the Estate of James Merrill.

1919

❦

D. H. Lawrence
["The deep sensual soul"]

Let us confess our belief: our deep, our religious belief. The great eternity of creation does not lie in the spirit, in the ideal. It lies in the everlasting and incalculable throb of passion and desire. The ideal is but the iridescence of the strange flux. Life does not begin in the mind: or in some ideal spirit. Life begins in the deep, the indescribable sensual throb of desire, pre-mental.

What is the soul, gentle reader? What is your soul, what is my soul? It is not some evaporated spirit. Ah no. It is that deep core of individual unity where life itself, the very God, throbs incalculably, whose throbbing unfolds the leaves and stem of the body, and brings forth the flower of the mind and the spirit. But the spirit is not the soul. Ah no. The soul has its deep fibrilled foliage in the damp earth, has its dark leaves in the air, it tosses the flower of the spirit like a bauble, a lovely plaything, on to the winds of time. Man can live without spirit or ideal, as dark pine-trees live without flowers: dark and sap-powerful. But without the deep sensual soul man is even inconceivable. This angel business, this spirit nonsense! Even spirits, such as really exist, are potent sensual entities.

If you would like to get at the secret of tree worship – Druid and Germanic, nay, universal – then realise the dark, sap-powerful, flowerless tree of the mindless, non-spiritual, sensual soul.

Gentle reader, our era has landed in the *cul de sac* of the spirit and the ideal. And I, poor darling, grope my way back to the tree of life, on which Jesus was crucified. He did so want to be a free, abstract spirit, like a thought. And he was crucified upon the tree of the eternal primal sensual soul, which is man's first and greatest being. Now I, gentle reader, love my tree. And if my mind, my spirit, my conscious consciousness blossom upon the tree of me for a little while, then sheds its petals and is gone, well, that is its affair. I don't like dried flowers, *immortels*. I love my tree. And the tree of life itself never dies, however many blossoms and leaves may fall and turn to dust. I place my immortality in the dark sap of life, stream of eternal blood. And as for my mind and spirit – this book, for example, all my books – I toss them out like so much transient tree-

211

blossom and foliaged leaves, on to the winds of time. The static, written-down eternity is nothing to me: or rather, it is only a lovely side-show, almost a bauble: but lovely. Yes I love it – the spirit, the mind, the ideal. But not primarily. The primal soul I see in the face of the donkey that is tied to my gate, and which shifts its long ears. The dark, sensual soul, and that gorgeous mystery of sensual individuality.

From *Mr. Noon,* by D. H. Lawrence, copyright 1934 by Frieda Lawrence, copyright © renewed 1962 by Angelo Ravagli and C. Montague Weekley, Executors of the Estate of Frieda Lawrence Ravagli. Used by permission of Viking Penguin, a division of Penguin Books USA Inc., and (for Canada) of Laurence Pollinger Limited.

ca. 1921

∾

George Sturt
["The death of Old England"]

One aspect of the death of Old England and of the replacement of the more primitive nation by an "organised" modern state was brought out forcibly and very disagreeably by the War against Germany. It was not only that one saw the beautiful fir-woods going down, though that was bad. The trees, cut into lengths, stripped of their bark and stacked in piles, gave to many an erst secluded hill-side a staring publicity. This or that quiet place, the home of peace, was turned into a ghastly battle-field, with the naked and maimed corpses of trees lying about. Bad enough, all this was. Still, trees might grow again; the hollows might recover their wood-land privacy and peace for other generations to enjoy. But what would never be recovered, because in fact War had found it already all but dead, was the earlier English understanding of timber, the local knowledge of it, the patriarchal traditions of handling it. Of old there had been a close relationship between the tree-clad country-side and the English who dwelt there. But now, the affection and the reverence bred of this – for it had been with something near to reverence that a true provincial beheld his native trees – was all but gone. A sort of greedy prostitution desecrated the ancient woods. All round me I saw and heard of things being done with a light heart that had always seemed to me wicked – things as painful to my sympathies as harnessing a carriage-horse to a heavy dray, or as pulling down a cathedral to get building-stone. I resented it; resented seeing the fair timber callously felled at the wrong time of year, cut up too soon, not "seasoned" at all. Perhaps the German sin had made all this imperative; yet it was none the less hateful. Not as waste only was it hateful: it was an outrage on the wisdom of our forefathers – a wanton insult put upon Old England, in her woods and forests.

The new needs were so different from the old. What had been prized once was prized no more. The newer vehicles, motor-drawn, were not expected to last longer than eight or ten years at the most; five years, oftener, found them obsolete, and therefore durability was hardly considered in the timber used for their construction. But it was otherwise in the earlier time, in the old-fashioned wheelwright's shop. Any piece of work had to last for years. Fashion, or invention, didn't affect it. So it was held a shame to have to do work twice over because the original material had been faulty; and I have known old-fashioned workmen refuse to use likely-looking timber because they held it to be unfit for the job.

And they knew. The skilled workman was the final judge. Under the plane (it is little used now) or under the axe (it is all but obsolete) timber disclosed qualities hardly to be found otherwise. My own eyes know because my own hands have felt, but I cannot teach an outsider, the difference between ash that is "tough as whipcord," and ash that is "frow as a carrot," or "doaty," or "biscuity." In oak, in beech, these differences are equally plain, yet only to those who have been initiated by practical work.

. . . .

Another matter the wheelwright buyer had to know about was the soil the timber grew on. Age-long tradition helped him here. I, for instance, knew from my father's telling, and he perhaps from his father's, that the best beech in the district came from such and such a quarter: that the very limbs from the elm in one park would yield good "stocks" (hubs for wheels); and that in a certain luxuriant valley the beautiful-looking oaks had grown too fast and when opened were too shaky to be used. Yet I didn't know (and paid for not knowing) that on the clay, in one hollow of Alice Holt, the oak had a nasty trick of going "foxy-hearted." I bought a small "parcel" of trees there. They looked well enough too in the yard until the winter, when the sawyers began to saw them open. But then – tree after tree, sound at the butt, began about two feet up to disclose the "foxy" middle, the rusty-looking pith like rotten string or rope running far up. I don't think my father or grandfather would have bought timber from that hollow. They knew "England" in a more intimate way.

Reprinted with the permission of Cambridge University Press from
The Wheelwright's Shop, by George Sturt, London.

1923

Robert Graves
An English Wood

This valley wood is pledged
To the set shape of things,
And reasonably hedged:
Here are no harpies fledged,
No rocs may clap their wings,
Nor gryphons wave their stings.
Here, poised in quietude,
Calm elementals brood
On the set shape of things:
They fend away alarms
From this green wood.
Here nothing is that harms –
No bulls with lungs of brass,
No toothed or spiny grass,
No tree whose clutching arms
Drink blood when travellers pass,
No mount of glass;
No bardic tongues unfold
Satires or charms.
Only, the lawns are soft,

The tree-stems, grave and old;
Slow branches sway aloft,
The evening air comes cold,
The sunset scatters gold.
Small grasses toss and bend,
Small pathways idly tend
Towards no fearful end.

Reprinted with the permission of Carcanet Press Ltd. from *Complete Poems of Robert Graves*, Volume I, edited by Dunstan Ward and Beryl Graves, 1995.

1923

D. H. Lawrence
["A tree, which is still Pan"]

In the days before man got too much separated off from the universe, he *was* Pan, along with all the rest.

As a tree still is. A strong-willed, powerful thing-in-itself, reaching up and reaching down. With a powerful will of its own it thrusts green hands and huge limbs at the light above, and sends huge legs and gripping toes down, down between the earth and rocks, to the earth's middle.

Here, on this little ranch under the Rocky Mountains, a big pine tree rises like a guardian spirit in front of the cabin where we live. Long, long ago the Indians blazed it. And the lightning, or the storm, has cut off its crest. Yet its column is always there, alive and changeless, alive and changing. The tree has its own aura of life. And in winter the snow slips off it, and in June it sprinkles down its little catkin-like pollen-tips, and it hisses in the wind, and it makes a silence within a silence. It is a great tree, under which the house is built. And the tree is still within the allness of Pan. At night, when the lamplight shines out of the window, the great trunk dimly shows, in the near darkness, like an Egyptian column, supporting some powerful mystery in the over-branching darkness. By day, it is just a tree.

It is just a tree. The chipmunks skelter a little way up it, the little black-

215

and-white birds, tree-creepers, walk quick as mice on its rough perpendicular, tapping; the blue jays throng on its branches, high up, at dawn, and in the afternoon you hear the faintest rustle of many little wild doves alighting in its upper remoteness. It is a tree, which is still Pan.

And we live beneath it, without noticing.

From *Pan In America,* by D. H. Lawrence, edited by Roberts and Moore, copyright © 1959, 1963, 1968 by the Estate of Frieda Lawrence Ravagli, from *Phoenix: Uncollected Papers of D. H. Lawrence* by D. H. Lawrence, edited by Roberts and Moore. Used by permission of Viking Penguin, a division of Penguin Books USA Inc., and (for Canada) of Laurence Pollinger Limited.

ca. 1924

~&~

Ernest Hemingway
[Nick falls asleep]

Nick kept his direction by the sun. He knew where he wanted to strike the river and he kept on through the pine plain, mounting small rises to see other rises ahead of him and sometimes from the top of a rise a great solid island of pines off to his right or his left. He broke off some sprigs of the heathery sweet fern, and put them under his pack straps. The chafing crushed it and he smelled it as he walked.

He was tired and very hot, walking across the uneven, shadeless pine plain. At any time he knew he could strike the river by turning off to his left. It could not be more than a mile away. But he kept on toward the north to hit the river as far upstream as he could go in one day's walking.

For some time as he walked Nick had been in sight of one of the big islands of pine standing out above the rolling high ground he was crossing. He dipped down and then as he came slowly up to the crest of the bridge he turned and made toward the pine trees.

There was no underbrush in the island of pine trees. The trunks of the trees went straight up or slanted toward each other. The trunks were straight and brown without branches. The branches were high above. Some interlocked to make a solid shadow on the brown forest floor.

Around the grove of trees was a bare space. It was brown and soft under-foot as Nick walked on it. This was the over-lapping of the pine needle floor, extending out beyond the width of the high branches. The trees had grown tall and the branches moved high, leaving in the sun this bare space they had once covered with shadow. Sharp at the edge of this exten-sion of the forest floor commenced the sweet fern.

Nick slipped off his pack and lay down in the shade. He lay on his back and looked up into the pine trees. His neck and back and the small of his back rested as he stretched. The earth felt good against his back. He looked up at the sky, through the branches, and then shut his eyes. He opened them and looked up again. There was a wind high up in the branches. He shut his eyes again and went to sleep.

From "Big, Two-Hearted River," Part I. Excerpted with permission of Scribner, a Division of Simon & Schuster, from *In Our Time,* by Ernest Hemingway. Copyright 1925 by Charles Scribner's Sons. Copyright renewed 1953 by Ernest Hemingway.

1925

W. B. Yeats

["O chestnut tree..."]

Labour is blossoming or dancing where
The body is not bruised to pleasure soul,
Nor beauty born out of its own despair,
Nor blear-eyed wisdom out of midnight oil.
O chestnut tree, great rooted blossomer,
Are you the leaf, the blossom or the bole?
O body swayed to music, O brightening glance,
How can we know the dancer from the dance?

From "Among School Children." Reprinted with the permission of Simon & Schuster from *The Poems of W. B. Yeats: A New Edition,* edited by Richard J. Finneran. Copyright 1928 by Macmillan Publishing Company. Copyright renewed © 1956 by Georgie Yeats.

1926

❨

W. B. Yeats

[A tribute to Lady Gregory]

I meditate upon a swallow's flight,
Upon an aged woman and her house,
A sycamore and lime tree lost in night
Although that western cloud is luminous,
Great works constructed there in nature's spite
For scholars and for poets after us,
Thoughts long knitted into a single thought,
A dance-like glory that those walls begot.

. . . .

Here, traveller, scholar, poet, take your stand
When all those rooms and passages are gone,
When nettles wave upon a shapeless mound
And saplings root among the broken stone,
And dedicate – eyes bent upon the ground,
Back turned upon the brightness of the sun
And all the sensuality of the shade –
A moment's memory to that laurelled head.

From "Coole Park, 1929."
Reprinted with the permission of Simon & Schuster from *The Poems of W. B. Yeats:
A New Edition,* edited by Richard J. Finneran. Copyright 1933 by Macmillan
Publishing Company; Copyright renewed © 1961 by Bertha Georgie Yeats.

1928

Thomas Hardy

Throwing A Tree:
New Forest

The two executioners stalk along over the knolls,
Bearing two axes with heavy heads shining and wide,
And a long limp two-handled saw toothed for cutting great boles,
And so they approach the proud tree that bears the death-mark on its
side.

Jackets doffed they swing axes and chop away just above ground,
And the chips fly about and lie white on the moss and fallen leaves;
Till a broad deep gash in the bark is hewn all the way round,
And one of them tries to hook upward a rope, which at last he achieves.

The saw then begins, till the top of the tall giant shivers:
The shivers are seen to grow greater each cut than before:
They edge out the saw, tug the rope; but the tree only quivers,
And kneeling and sawing again, they step back to try pulling once more.

Then, lastly, the living mast sways, further sways: with a shout
Job and Ike rush aside. Reached the end of its long staying powers
The tree crashes downward: it shakes all its neighbours throughout,
And two hundred years' steady growth has been ended in less than two
hours.

Throwing a Tree: New Forest, by Thomas Hardy, London, Macmillan.

1928

Roy Campbell
Autumn

I love to see, when leaves depart,
The clear anatomy arrive,
Winter, the paragon of art,
That kills all forms of life and feeling
Save what is pure and will survive.

Already now the clanging chains
Of geese are harnessed to the moon:
Stripped are the great sun-clouding planes:
And the dark pines, their own revealing,
Let in the needles of the noon.

Strained by the gale the olives whiten
Like hoary wrestlers bent with toil
And, with the vines, their branches lighten
To brim our vats where summer lingers
In the red froth and sun-gold oil.

Soon on our hearth's reviving pyre
Their rotted stems will crumble up:
And like a ruby, panting fire,
The grape will redden on your fingers
Through the lit crystal of the cup.

Reprinted with the permission of Francisco Campbell Custodio
and Ad Donker Publishers.

1930

"The William Wilberforce oak at Keston, with the inscription on the seat," photograph. Published in William Wilberforce: The Story of a Great Crusade, *by Travers Buxton, London, The Religious Tract Society.*

1933

꧁

Ernst Toller
["The dead and the living"]

A devastated wood; miserable words. A tree is like a human being. The sun shines on it. It has roots, and the roots thrust down into the earth; the rain waters it, and the wind stirs its branches. It grows, and it dies. And we know little about its growth and still less about its death. It bows to the autumn gales, but it is not death that comes then; only the reviving sleep of winter.

A forest is like a people. A devastated forest is like a massacred people. The limbless trunks stare blackly at the day; even merciful night cannot veil them; even the wind is cold and alien.

Through one of those devastated woods which crept like a fester across Europe ran the French and German trenches. We lay so close to each other that if we had stuck our heads over the parapet we could have talked to each other without raising our voices.

We slept huddled together in sodden dugouts, where the water trickled down the walls and the rats gnawed at our bread and our sleep was troubled with dreams of home and war. One day there would be nine of us, the next only eight. We did not bury our dead. We pushed them into the little niches in the wall of the trench cut as resting places for ourselves. When I went slipping and slithering down the trench, with my head bent low, I did not know whether the men I passed were dead or alive; in that place the dead and the living had the same gray faces.

From *I Was A German,* by Ernst Toller, translated by Edward Crankshaw (from the German *Eine Jugend In Deutschland*), London, The Bodley Head.

1934

◌∿

William Faulkner
["Brooding and inscrutable impenetrability"]

Then, his old hammer double gun which was only twelve years younger than he standing between his knees, he watched even the last puny marks of man – cabin, clearing, the small and irregular fields which a year ago were jungle and in which the skeleton stalks of this year's cotton stood almost as tall and rank as the old cane had stood, as if man had had to marry his planting to the wilderness in order to conquer it – fall away and vanish. The twin banks marched with wilderness as he remembered it – the tangle of brier and cane impenetrable even to sight twenty feet away, the tall tremendous soaring of oak and gum and ash and hickory which had rung to no axe save the hunter's, had echoed to no machinery save the beat of old-time steam boats traversing it or to the snarling of launches like their own of people going into it to dwell for a week or two weeks because it was still wilderness. There was some of it left, although now it was two hundred miles from Jefferson when once it had been thirty. He had watched it, not being conquered, destroyed, so much as retreating since its purpose was served now and its time an outmoded time, retreating southward through this inverted-apex, this V-shaped section of earth between hills and River until what was left of it seemed now to be gathered and for the time arrested in one tremendous density of brooding and inscrutable impenetrability at the ultimate funnelling tip.

From "Delta Autumn," *Go Down, Moses,* by William Faulkner. Copyright © 1942 by William Faulkner. Reprinted by permission of Random House, Inc.

1942

✿

Willa Cather

[On a little island off the Nova Scotia coast]

He hurried out of the kitchen door and up the grassy hillside to the spruce wood. The spruces stood tall and still as ever in the morning air; the same dazzling spears of sunlight shot through their darkness. The path underneath had the dampness, the magical softness which his feet remembered. On either side of the trail yellow toadstools and white mushrooms lifted the heavy thatch of brown spruce needles and made little damp tents. Everything was still in the wood.

There was not a breath of wind; deep shadow and new-born light, yellow as gold, a little unsteady like other new-born things. It was blinking, too, as if its own reflection on the dewdrops was too bright. Or maybe the light had been asleep down under the sea and was just waking up.

"Hello, Grandfather!" Grenfell cried as he turned a curve in the path. The grandfather was a giant spruce tree that had been struck by lightning (must have been about a hundred years ago, the islanders said). It still lay on a slant along a steep hillside, its shallow roots in the air, all its great branches bleached grayish white, like an animal skeleton long exposed to the weather. Grenfell put out his hand to twitch off a twig as he passed, but it snapped back at him like a metal spring. He stopped in astonishment, his hand smarted, actually.

"Well, Grandfather! Lasting pretty well, I should say. Compliments! You get good drainage on this hillside, don't you?"

Ten minutes more on the winding uphill path brought him to the edge of the spruce wood and out on a bald headland that topped a cliff two hundred feet above the sea. He sat down on a rock and grinned.

. . . .

Grenfell shook himself and hurried along up the cliff trail. He crossed the first brook on stepping-stones. Must have been recent rain, for the water was rushing down the deep-cut channel with sound and fury till it leaped hundreds of feet over the face of the cliff and fell into the sea: a white waterfall that never rested.

The trail led on through a long jungle of black alder then through a lazy, rooty, brown swamp … and then out on another breezy, grassy headland which jutted far out into the air in a horseshoe curve. There one could stand beside a bushy rowan tree and see four waterfalls, white as silver, pouring down the perpendicular cliff walls.

Nothing had changed. Everything was the same, and he, Henry Grenfell, was the same: the relationship was unchanged. Not even a tree blown down; the stunted beeches (precious because so few) were still holding out against a climate unkind to them. The old white birches that grew on the edge of the cliff had been so long beaten and tormented by east wind and north wind that they grew more down than up, and hugged the earth that was kinder than the stormy air. Their growth was all one-sided, away from the sea, and their land-side branches actually lay along the ground and crept up the hillside through the underbrush, persistent, nearly naked, like great creeping vines, and at last, when they got into the sunshine, burst into tender leafage.

This knob of grassy headland with the bushy rowan tree had been his vague objective when he left the cabin. From this elbow he could look back on the cliff wall, both north and south, and see the four silver waterfalls in the morning light. A splendid sight, Grenfell was thinking, and all his own.

From "Before Breakfast," *The Old Beauty and Others*, by Willa Cather. Copyright 1948 by Alfred A. Knopf Inc. Reprinted by permission of the publisher.

1944

∾

Evelyn Waugh
["Two realities and two dreams"]

Outside the hut I stood awed and bemused between two realities and two dreams. The rain had ceased but the clouds hung low and heavy overhead. It was a still morning and the smoke from the cookhouse rose straight to the leaden sky. A cart-track, once metalled, then overgrown, now rutted and churned to mud, followed the contour of the hillside and dipped out of sight below a knoll, and on either side of it lay the haphazard litter of corrugated iron, from which rose the rattle and chatter and whistling and catcalls, all the zoo-noises of the battalion beginning a new day. Beyond and about us, more familiar still, lay an exquisite man-made landscape. It was a sequestered place, enclosed and embraced in a single, winding valley. Our camp lay along one gentle slope; opposite us the ground led, still unravished, to the neighbourly horizon, and between us flowed a stream – it was named the Bride and rose not two miles away at a farm called Bridesprings, where we used sometimes to walk to tea; it became a considerable river lower down before it joined the Avon – which had been dammed here to form three lakes, one no more than a wet slate among the reeds, but the others more spacious, reflecting the clouds and the mighty beeches at their margin. The woods were all of oak and beech, the oak grey and bare, the beech faintly dusted with green by the breaking buds; they made a simple, carefully designed pattern with the green glades and the wide green spaces – Did the fallow deer graze here still? – and, lest the eye wander aimlessly, a Doric temple stood by the water's edge, and an ivy-grown arch spanned the lowest of the connecting weirs. All this had been planned and planted a century and a half ago so that, at about this date, it might be seen in its maturity. From where I stood the house was hidden by a green spur, but I knew well how and where it lay, couched among the lime trees like a hind in the bracken. Which was the mirage, which the palpable earth?

Reprinted with the permission of The Peters Fraser & Dunlop Group on behalf of the Evelyn Waugh Estate, from the Prologue to *Brideshead Revisited*, by Evelyn Waugh, London, Chapman and Hall.

1944

☾

Philip Larkin
["Time"]

This is the first thing
I have understood:
Time is the echo of an axe
Within a wood.

The North Ship, XXVI.
From *Collected Poems* by Philip Larkin. Copyright © 1988, 1989 by the Estate of
Philip Larkin. Reprinted with permission of Farrar, Straus & Giroux, Inc.

1945

Emily Carr
["A dream of greenery"]

These windows let in an extensive view, a view of housetops, trees, sea, purple mountains and sky. The view seemed to come companionably into the room rather than to draw me out; and it had an additional glory, but for this glory you must look *out*, look *down*. Then you saw right into the heart of a great Western maple tree. Its huge bole culminated in widespread, stout branches. There was room for immense life in this bole.

The maple tree was always beautiful, always gracious. In spring it had a sunlit, pale-yellow glory, in summer it was deep, restful green, in autumn it was gold and bronze, in winter it was a gnarled network of branches. It was in winter you saw best the tree's reality, its build-up and strength.

On the whitewashed underside of the roof shingles of my attic room I painted two immense totemic Indian eagles. Their outstretched wings covered the entire ceiling. They were brave birds, powerful of beak and talon. Their plumage was indicated in the Indian way – a few carefully studied feathers painted on wing, breast, and tail gave the impression that the bird was fully plumed.

Sleeping beneath these two strong birds, the stout Western maple tree beneath my window, is it wonder that I should have strong dreams, dreams that folded me very close!

One night I had a dream of greenery. I never attacked the painting of growing foliage quite the same after that dream I think; growing green had become something different to me.

In my dream I saw a wooded hillside, an ordinary slope such as one might see along any Western roadside, tree-covered, normal, no particular pattern or design to catch an artist's eye were he seeking subject-matter. But, in my dream that hillside suddenly lived – weighted with sap, burning green in every leaf, every scrap of it vital!

Woods, that had always meant so much to me, from that moment meant just so much more.

From "Green," *Growing Pains: The Autobiography of Emily Carr*, Toronto,
Oxford University Press.

1946

Earle Birney
From the Hazel Bough

He met a lady
    on a lazy street
hazel eyes
    and little plush feet

her legs swam by
    like lovely trout
eyes were trees
    where boys leant out

hands in the dark and
    a river side
round breasts rising
    with the finger's tide

she was plump as a finch
    and live as a salmon
gay as silk and
    proud as a Brahmin

they winked when they met
    and laughed when they parted
never took time
    to be broken-hearted

but no man sees
    where the trout lie now
or what leans out
    from the hazel bough

From *Ghost In The Wheels*, by Earle Birney. Used by permission of McClelland & Stewart, Inc., Toronto, *The Canadian Publishers*.

1945-47

J. R. R. Tolkien

[Niggle's picture]

Niggle was a painter. Not a very successful one, partly because he had many other things to do.

....

He had a number of pictures on hand; most of them were too large and ambitious for his skill. He was the sort of painter who can paint leaves better than trees. He used to spend a long time on a single leaf, trying to catch its shape, and its sheen, and the glistening of dewdrops on its edges. Yet he wanted to paint a whole tree, with all of its leaves in the same style, and all of them different.

There was one picture in particular which bothered him. It had begun with a leaf caught in the wind, and it became a tree; and the tree grew, sending out innumerable branches, and thrusting out the most fantastic roots. Strange birds came and settled on the twigs and had to be attended to. Then all round the Tree, and behind it, through the gaps in the leaves and boughs, a country began to open out; and there were glimpses of a forest marching over the land, and of mountains tipped with snow. Niggle lost interest in his other pictures; or else he took them and tacked them on to the edges of his great picture. Soon the canvas became so large that he had to get a ladder; and he ran up and down it, putting in a touch here, and rubbing out a patch there. When people came to call, he seemed polite enough, though he fiddled a little with the pencils on his desk. He listened to what they said, but underneath he was thinking all the time about his big canvas, in the tall shed that had been built for it out in his garden (on a plot where once he had grown potatoes).

Reprinted with the permission of Harper Collins Publishers Ltd. From "Leaf by Niggle," *Tree and Leaf*, by J. R. R. Tolkien, London, George Allen and Unwin.

1947

Ernest Buckler

[The Annapolis Valley and the mountains]

David Canaan had lived in Entremont all his thirty years. As far back as childhood, whenever anger had dishevelled him, or confusion, or the tick, tick, tick, of emptiness like he felt today, he had sought the log road that went to the top of the mountain....

He stood at the kitchen window now, watching the highway.

The highway was irregularly noduled with whitewashed wooden houses. It cut through the Annapolis Valley; and on either side of it lay the flat frozen fields.

On the north side, the fields and orchards ran down to the big bend of the river, cut wide by the Fundy tides. Blocks of grimy, sun-eaten ice were piled up in Druidic formations on the river's banks, where the tides had tumbled them. The North Mountain rose sharply beyond the river. It was solid blue in the afternoon light of December that was pale and sharp as starlight, except for the milky ways of choppings where traces of the first snow never quite disappeared.

On the south side of the highway, beyond the barn and the pastures, the South Mountain rose. Solid blue too at the bottom where the dark spruces huddled close, but snow-grey higher up where the sudden steepness and the leafless hardwood began. At the peak the gaunt limbs of the maples could be seen like the bones of hands all along the lemon-coloured horizon.

The mountain slopes were less than a mile high at their topmost point but they shut the valley in completely.

From *The Mountain and the Valley,* by Ernest Buckler. Used by permission of McClelland & Stewart, Inc., Toronto, *The Canadian Publishers.*

1952

Margaret Laurence
["That house in Manawaka"]

That house in Manawaka is the one which, more than any other, I carry with me. Known to the rest of the town as "the old Connor place" and to the family as the Brick House, it was plain as the winter turnips in its root cellar, sparsely windowed as some crusader's embattled fortress in a heathen wilderness, its rooms in a perpetual gloom except in the brief height of summer. Many other brick structures had existed in Manawaka for as much as half a century, but at the time when my grandfather built his house, part dwelling place and part massive monument, it had been the first of its kind.

Set back at a decent distance from the street, it was screened by a line of spruce trees whose green-black branches swept down to the earth like the sternly protective wings of giant hawks. Spruce was not indigenous to that part of the prairies. Timothy Connor had brought the seedlings all the way from Galloping Mountain, a hundred miles north, not on whim, one may be sure, but feeling that they were the trees for him. By the mid-thirties, the spruces were taller than the house, and two generations of children had clutched at boughs which were as rough and hornily knuckled as the hands of old farmers, and had swung themselves up to secret sanctuaries. On the lawn a few wild blue violets dared to grow, despite frequent beheadings from the clanking guillotine lawn mower, and mauve-flowered Creeping Charley insinuated deceptively weak-looking tendrils up to the very edges of the flower beds where helmeted snapdragon stood in precision.

From "The Sound of the Singing," *A Bird in the House,* by Margaret Laurence. Used by permission (for Canada) of McClelland & Stewart, Inc., *The Canadian Publishers.* (In the United States) © 1963 by Margaret Laurence. Reprinted with the permission of New End Inc.

1963

◆

Robert Lowell
["The round slice of an oak"]

On my pilgrimage to Northampton,
I found no relic,
except the round slice of an oak
you are said to have planted.

It was flesh-colored, new,
and a common piece of kindling,
only fit for burning.
You too must have been green once.

From "Jonathan Edwards in Western Massachusetts," *Selected Poems,* by Robert Lowell. Copyright © 1976 by Robert Lowell. Reprinted by permission of Farrar, Straus & Giroux, Inc.

1964

W. K. Thomas
["The poplars Cowper lost are here"]

The poplars Cowper lost are here,
a noble line of sparkling shade,
with rustling whispers, calm and clear,
a towering, living colonnade.

The breathing quiet Arnold heard
is here beside this island grove,
with girdling city noises blurred
like distant breakers round a cove.

At hand, like Yeats's salmon leaping,
the flash of falls through cut-leaf screening;
beyond, the shouts of children leaping
and scream of peacock proudly preening.

But here a pulsing calm that grows
with whispers from the silver leaves,
of pioneers and sturdy rows
of summer children stooking sheaves.

Come, walk with me and we shall trace,
here through the park, how hand
by hand our pioneering race
first cleared, enriched, then built this land.

Begin where Hurons threaded through,
in woods grown dense with underbrush,
where bracken fronds obstruct the view,
cicada's shrilling breaks the hush.

There fungus circles swell, oaks spread,
white, peeling birches slash the sky,
while maples, elms meet overhead –
a tangled frieze that fills the eye.

Step through, to a grassland sweep,
where slashing, stumping, burning's done,
the stones pulled off, the stakes set deep,
where sowing, reaping's come and gone,

where, peaceful now, the pastures slope
to the winding creek where cattle stood
in rippling rushes green and taupe,
against a Homer Watson wood.

Walk up the gentle hill; pass near
these poplars, trembling in repose,
and see McArthur sitting here,
head tilted, busy, hunting crows.

Pass on to where a road takes form,
where wild flowers, weeds, and grass conceal
some relics – see a groundhog swarm
through spokes of a wagon's iron-shod wheel.

Cross rails deep rusted with disuse,
pass square-cut timbers felled in their prime,
abandoned now, dark brown and puce,
glistening with creosote and time.

. . . .

All of a piece, each boy who broke
new ground, however hard, like squill,
each worker with the steady drive
to flourish higher, like the oak,
each forebear with the stubborn will
the poplars have, to grow and thrive.

Reprinted with the permission of W. K. Thomas from "Waterloo Park,"
by W. K. Thomas, *Copperfield* 2 (Spring 1970).

1970

~

Louis Dudek

Tree in a Street

Why will not that tree adapt itself to our tempo?
We have lopped off several branches,
cut her skin to the white bone,
run wires through her body and her loins,
yet she will not change.
Ignorant of traffic, of dynamos and steel,
as uncontemporary
as bloomers and bustles
she stands there like a green cliché.

Reprinted with the permission of Louis Dudek. From *Collected Poetry*.

1971

ℬ

Daisaku Ikeda

[The Buddha and the Bodhi tree]

Various sources identify the place where Shakyamuni [the Buddha] gained enlightenment as the town of Gaya in Uruvela, not far from the village of Sena. Because of this it has come to be called Buddh Gaya, and there is a temple there today. In similar fashion, the large tree under which Shakyamuni was seated when he gained enlightenment came to be called the Bodhi tree, or Tree of Enlightenment. It was of the variety known as *ashvattha*, or pipal fig, which seems to have grown widely in various parts of India.

Meditating under a tree appears to have been a custom among the Indian ascetics of Shakyamuni's time. Buddhist scriptures and other writings make frequent mention of ascetics sitting in the quiet shade of a tree and practicing contemplation in hopes of grasping the nature of the in-

235

ner self or of ultimate reality. The pipal tree in particular, with its widespread roots and luxuriant foliage, was from early times looked upon as holy and was regarded as providing a worthy place for the contemplation of immortality. It is not surprising, therefore, that Shakyamuni should have chosen this kind of tree to sit beneath when he embarked upon the last stage of his search for enlightenment. Even today in Buddh Gaya there is a large pipal or Bodhi tree, though no claim is made that it is actually the tree under which Shakyamuni sat.

. . . .

Shakyamuni seated himself on the mat under the pipal tree, determined to win enlightenment. He assumed the so-called lotus posture, which was the usual way of sitting in yoga, and meditational practices. In this posture the legs are crossed, the feet placed soles upward on the opposite thighs; the hands rest on the lap, the left over the right, palms upward and thumbs touching. This was regarded as the most stable and desirable position for sitting.

. . . .

Shakyamuni's enlightenment took place at dawn, or, as it is customarily described in the scriptures, "when the morning star appeared." Under the Bodhi tree he sat in deep meditation as the night wore on. With the approach of dawn, the eye of his wisdom gained sublime clarity, and when the morning star began to shine, he sensed his life bursting open and in a flash discerned the ultimate reality of things. In that moment of enlightenment he became a Buddha, and the Buddhist faith, which was to have such an immeasurable impact upon the history of mankind, was born.

Reprinted with the permission of Weatherhill Inc. from *The Living Buddha*, by Daisaku Ikeda, translated by Burton Watson, New York, Weatherhill Inc., 1976.

1973

Philip Larkin
The Trees

The trees are coming into leaf
Like something almost being said;
The recent buds relax and spread,
Their greenness is a kind of grief.

Is it that they are born again
And we grow old? No, they die too.
Their yearly trick of looking new
Is written down in rings of grain.

Yet still the unresting castles thresh
In fullgrown thickness every May.
Last year is dead, they seem to say,
Begin afresh, afresh, afresh.

From *Collected Poems,* by Philip Larkin. Copyright © 1988, 1989 by the Estate of
Philip Larkin. Reprinted by permission of Farrar, Straus & Giroux, Inc.

1974

ॐ

Anonymous
Fireplace Logs

Beech wood logs are bright and clear,
If the logs are kept a year.
Chestnut's only good they say
If for long it's laid away.
Birch and fir logs burn too fast,
Blaze up quick but do not last;
Elm wood burns like churchyard mould –
E'en the very flames are cold.
Poplar gives a bitter smoke,
Fills your eyes and makes you choke.
Apple wood will scent your room
With an incense like perfume.
Oak and maple, if dry and old,
Keep away the winter cold.
But ash wood wet, or ash wood dry,
A king can warm his slippers by.

From a broadcast on CBC Radio (CBL, Toronto), January 13, 1974.

1974

&

John Fowles

["The natural aura of certain woodland or forest settings"]

We know that the very first holy places in Neolithic times, long before Stonehenge (which is only a petrified copse), were artificial wooden groves made of felled, transported and re-erected tree trunks; and that their roofs must have seemed to their makers less roofs than artificial leaf-canopies. Even the smallest woods have their secrets and secret places, their unmarked precincts, and I am certain all sacred buildings, from the greatest cathedral to the smallest chapel, and in all religions, derive from the natural aura of certain woodland or forest settings. In them we stand among older, larger and infinitely other beings, remoter from us than the most bizarre other non-human forms of life: blind, immobile, speechless (or speaking only Baudelaire's *confuses paroles*), waiting...altogether very like the only form a universal god could conceivably take. The Neolithic peoples, the slaves, as we are of an industrial economy, of their own great new cultural "invention" of farming, were the first great deforesters of our landscapes, and perhaps it was guilt that made them return to the trees to find a model for their religious buildings – in which they were followed by the Bronze Age, the Greeks and Romans with their columns and porticoes, the Celtic Iron Age with its Druids and sacred oak-groves.

From *The Tree*, by John Fowles. Text and English translation copyright © 1979 by Association for All Speech Impaired Children (AFASIC). By permission of Little, Brown and Company.

1979

John Fowles
[Wistman's Wood]

Wistman's Wood may be obscurely sited, but it is no longer, as it was in the 1940s, obscurely known. The rise of ecology has seen to that. In scientific terms it is an infinitely rare fragment of primeval forest, from some warmer phase of world climate, that has managed to cling on – though not without some remarkable adaptations – in this inhospitable place; and even more miraculously managed to survive the many centuries of human depredation of anything burnable on the Moor. Culturally it is comparable with a great Neolithic site: a sort of Avebury of the tree, an *Ur*-wood. Physically it is a half-mile chain of copses splashed, green drops in a tachist painting, along what on Dartmoor they call a clitter, a broken debris of granite boulders – though not at all on true tachist principle, by chance. These boulders provide the essential protection for seedlings against bitter winter winds and grazing sheep. But the real ecological miracle of Wistman's Wood is botanical. Its dominant species, an essentially lowland one, should not really be here at all, and is found at this altitude in only one other, and Irish, site in the British Isles. Here and there in the wood are a scatter of mountain ashes, a few hollies. But the reigning tree is the ancient king of all our trees: *Quercus robur*, the Common, or English, Oak.

We go down, to the uppermost brink. Names, science, history…not even the most adamantly down-to-earth botanist thinks of species and ecologies when he or she first stands at Wistman's Wood. It is too strange for that. The normal full-grown height of the common oak is thirty to forty metres. Here the very largest, and even though they are centuries old, rarely top five metres. They are just coming into leaf, long after their lowland kin, in every shade from yellow-green to bronze. Their dark branches grow to an extraordinary extent laterally; are endlessly angled, twisted, raked, interlocked, and reach quite as much downward as upwards. These trees are inconceivably different from the normal habit of their species, far more like specimens from a natural bonzai nursery. They seem, even though the day is windless, to be writhing, convulsed, each its own Laocoön, caught and frozen in some fanatically private struggle for existence.

The next thing one notices is even more extraordinary, in this Ice Age environment. It is a paradoxically tropical quality, for every lateral branch, fork, saddle of these aged dwarfs is densely clothed in other plants – not just the tough little polypodies of most deciduous woodlands, but large, elegantly pluming male ferns; whortleberry beds, grasses, huge cushions of moss and festoons of lichen. The clitter of granite boulders, bare on the windswept moors, here provides a tumbling and chaotic floor of moss-covered mounds and humps, which add both to the impression of frozen movement and to that of an astounding internal fertility, since they seem to stain the upward air with their vivid green. This floor like a tilted emerald sea, the contorted trunks, the interlacing branches with their luxuriant secondary aerial gardens ... there is only one true epithet to convey the first sight of Wistman's Wood, even today. It is fairy-like. It corresponds uncannily with the kind of setting artists like Richard Dadd imagined for that world in Victorian times and have now indelibly given it: teeming, jewel-like, self-involved, rich in secrets just below the threshold of our adult human senses.

We enter. The place has an intense stillness, as if here the plant side of creation rules and even birds are banned; below, through the intricate green gladelets and branch-gardens, comes the rush of water in a moorland stream, one day to join the sea far to the south. This water-noise, like the snore of the raven again, the breeding-trill of a distant curlew, seems to come from another world, once one is inside the wood. There are birds, of course...an invisible hedgesparrow, its song not lost here, as it usually is, among all the sounds of other common garden birds, nor lost in its own ubiquity in Britain; but piercing and peremptory, individual, irretrievable; even though, a minute later, we hear its *prestissimo* bulbul shrill burst out again. My wood, my wood, it never shall be yours.

From *The Tree,* by John Fowles. Text and English translation copyright © 1979 by Association for All Speech Impaired Children (AFASIC). By permission of Little, Brown and Company.

1979

‹❦›

Alice Munro
[Woodcraft]

This fall the demand for wood was greater than ever, and Roy was going out two or three times in a week. Most people recognize trees by their leaves or by their general shape and size, but Roy, walking in the leafless deep bush, knows them by their bark. Ironwood, that heavy and reliable firewood, has a shaggy brown bark on its stocky trunk, but its limbs are smooth at their tips and decidedly reddish. Cherry is the blackest tree in the bush, and the bark lies in neat scales. Most people would be surprised at how high the cherry trees grow in the bush; they are nothing like orchard trees there. Apple trees are not so tall, or so dark, or so definitely scaled, but their wood burns for a long time and smells sweet. Ash is a soldierly tree – straight, corduroy-ribbed columns. Maple has a gray bark with irregular roughness, the shadows making black streaks; there is some comfortable carelessness about these streaks and shadows – which meet sometimes in rough rectangles, sometimes not – that is suitable to the maple, which is homely and familiar and what everybody thinks of when they think of a tree. Beech trees and oak are another matter; there is something notable and dramatic about them, though neither is so lovely in shape as the elm trees, which are gone. Beech has the smooth gray bark that is usually chosen for the carving of initials. These carvings widen with the years, the decades, from the knife's slim groove to blotches that make the letters wider than long. Beech will grow a hundred feet high in the bush. In the open they spread out – they are as wide as high – but in the bush they shoot up, and then the limbs at the top will take radical turns; they look like stag horns. But this arrogant-looking tree can have a weakness of twisted grain, which can be detected by ripples in the bark. That is a sign that it may break, or go down in a high wind. As for oak trees, they are not common in this country, not so common as beech, and always easy to spot. Just as maple trees always look like the common, necessary tree in the back yard, so oak trees look like trees in storybooks, as if in all the stories that begin "Once upon a time on the edge of the woods," the woods were full of oak trees. Their dark, shiny, elaborately indented leaves contribute to this look, but they are just as remarkable when the leaves are off and they show their thick corky bark, with its gray-black color and intricate surface, and the elaborate twisting and curling of their branches.

Roy thinks that there is very little danger in going tree cutting alone if you know what you are doing. When you are going to cut down a tree, the first thing is to assess its center of gravity, then cut a seventy-degree wedge, so that the center of gravity is just over it. The side the wedge is on, of course, determines the direction in which the tree will fall. You make a falling cut, from the opposite side, not to connect with the wedge cut but in line with its high point. The idea is to cut through the tree, leaving at the end a hinge of wood which is the very center of the tree's weight and from which it must fall. It is best to make it fall clear of all other branches, but sometimes there is no way this can happen. If a tree is leaning into the branches of other trees, and you can't get a truck into position to haul it out with a chain, you cut the trunk in sections from beneath, till the upper part drops free and falls. When you've dropped a tree and it's resting on its branches, you get the trunk to the ground by cutting through the limb wood until you find the limbs that are holding it up. These limbs are under pressure – they may be bent like a bow – and the trick is to cut so that the trunk will roll away from you and the limbs won't whack you. When it is safely down, you cut the trunk into stove lengths, and split the stove lengths with the axe. Sometimes there's a surprise. Some squirrelly wood blocks can't be split with the axe; they have to be laid on their sides and ripped with a chain saw; the sawdust cut this way, with the grain, is ripped away in long shreds. Also, some beech or maple has to be sidesplit, the great round chunk cut along the growth rings on all sides until it is almost square and can be more easily attacked. Sometimes there's dozy wood, in which a fungus has grown inside, between the rings. But in general the toughness of the blocks is as you'd expect: greater in the body wood than in the limb wood, and greater in the broad trunks that have grown up in the open than in the tall, slim ones that have pushed up in the middle of the bush.

Roy's thoughts about wood are covetous and nearly obsessive, though he has never been a greedy man in any other way. He can lie awake nights thinking of a splendid beech he wants to get at. He thinks of all the woodlots in the county that he has never even seen, because they are hidden at the back of farms. If he is driving along a road that goes through a bush, he swings his head from side to side, afraid of missing something.

Even what is worthless for his purposes will interest him; for instance, a stand of blue beech, too delicate, too weedy to bother with. He sees the dark, vertical ribs slanting down the paler trunks; he remembers where they are. He would like to map every bush he sees, get it in his mind, know what is there.

From "Wood," originally published in the November 24, 1980, issue of *The New Yorker*. Reprinted by arrangement with the Virginia Barber Literary Agency. All rights reserved.

1980

❧

Andrew Revkin
[Amazonia]

Xapuri and the hundreds of other human settlements in the Amazon are like tiny islands scattered in a great green sea. Some are linked by roads cut through the wilderness; others can be reached only by boat or airplane. Even Manaus, once the gleaming center of the rubber boom and now a noisy, polluted city of 700,000, is like an island, connected by only one road to the developed south of Brazil. Overall, despite the devastation around the edges and the fishbone pattern of open space that eats into the trees wherever a network of roads is built, the overwhelming majority of the region remains virgin forest. From above, it seems to be a uniformly mottled green carpet, touched here and there with pink or rust or yellow where a particular tree species is in flower. On a thousand-mile flight over the underdeveloped parts of the basin, you look down on nothing but that carpet, the only distraction being the occasional glint of the rivers, which coil and twist like a spilled spool of silver ribbon, or here and there a clearing where an Indian tribe or rubber tapper community has carved out a small patch in which to raise crops.

....

The flooded forest is an ecosystem all its own, where plants must survive for months underwater and fishes swim for part of the year through the treetops, eating fruit and playing an important role in distributing seeds. The *terra firme*, firm ground, that makes up the rest of Amazonia tends to have aged soils that have been washed clean of nutrients over millennia. In some areas, there is natural savanna, in others, low forests that are little more than a tangle of lianas. But huge swathes of *terra firme* support rich rain forest. This forest has evolved in such a way that it is nearly independent of the substrate. The system feeds itself and waters itself, recycling nutrients and holding water in its biomass like an enormous sponge. It is somewhat like hydroponic agriculture, in which plants can thrive on sterile sand – or even suspended in racks – as long as they receive moisture, nutrients, carbon dioxide, and sunlight.

Within any single patch of rain forest, there is also an initial impression of monotony: all you see are columnar trunks, thickets of vines and creepers, mats of decaying leaves. It is only after you have walked for a while in a mature stand of rain forest that individual elements begin to stand out: trees with flying buttresses, hanging plants, climbing plants, plants with fruit clustered high in the air, or plants – like cocoa – in which the fruit grows directly out of the tree trunk. You notice that your feet are intermittently shuffling through foot-long canoe-shape leaves, then plate-size hand-shape leaves, then a dusting of purple flower petals dropping from unseen blossoms 100 feet above. A Morpho butterfly flits past, like an animated origami masterpiece folded from a sheet of electric-blue foil (one naturalist described these seven-inch forest dwellers as "the bluest things in the world"). As you walk on, a tree above you clacks quietly in the wind and a woody pod falls at your feet. It is the seed pod of *Cariniana micrantha*, a relative of the Brazil nut. Out of its end pops a perfectly fitted cap. In the exposed cavity you see tightly packed regiments of seeds, each with a feathery tail that would have allowed it to soar away from the parent tree – if the monkey that dropped the seed pod had left it on the tree to ripen a little longer.

The dizzying complexity of the forest exists at all levels. Every time you turn to focus on a particular object, perhaps a rotting log, that object then splits into individual elements – fungi, beetles, ants, and a pile of aromatic wood dust where a nest of termites has been hard at work. Look even more closely, and those fragments would split apart yet again. The leaf-cutter ants crossing the log are carrying chunks of plant material into their subterranean fungus garden. Spores of the fungus are planted on its food source, and later the ants harvest the fruiting bodies that the fungi produce. The ants cannot digest the leaves themselves, and the fungi have evolved to an extent that they can no longer live anywhere but in nests watched over by ants. Meanwhile, the termites' guts harbor bacteria without which they cannot digest the tough cellulose skeleton of the tree. The beetles are attacking a pile of monkey droppings. And, at the point where the log appears to be slowly sinking into the earth, a thick mat of fungal threads called mycorrhizae are reducing the dead wood to its chemical constituents. These constituents include traces of minerals such as phosphorus, a coveted commodity in Amazon forests.

The fungi have a symbiotic relationship with the surrounding trees, and if you were able to trace the strings from which that fungal mat is woven, you would see that they emanate from nearby shallow tree roots. Although the fungi are a separate organism from the tree, neither can thrive without the other. Where the fungus interlaces with the tissue of the tree root, there is an ongoing exchange of goods. The tree provides the fungus with carbon-based compounds that help it grow, and the fungus provides the tree with recycled phosphorus and other minerals. Slowly, as you absorb more and more of the details around you, the spectacular complexity and interrelatedness of the rain forest become overwhelmingly apparent.

Even so, that which can be seen at eye level or on the forest floor is just a taste of the richness of the forest. It is in the canopy – the topmost layers of branches and foliage 100 feet or more above the floor – that the incredible biological bounty is most apparent. Many researchers have noted the similarity between tropical rain forests and coral reefs. In both ecosystems, life occurs in strata, with the richest array of life forms in the layer closest to the sun. In the case of a coral reef, that is the shallowest part, where innumerable fishes and invertebrates rely for their food on phytoplankton and corals sustained by photosynthesis. In the rain forest, it is the canopy. This stratum has been called the last great unexplored frontier of the natural world. While the coral reef has been made accessible by scuba gear, there is still no simple way to wander through the treetops. In the shadows beneath the canopy, less and less grows and thrives until finally – on the equivalent of the deep sea floor, where little light penetrates – there is the thin brown layer of rotting mulch and the tangle of runners and buttressed tree roots, much of which is simply there to support the rich community far above.

The forest's layered look has been determined by the location of the crucial fuels that it needs to thrive. The architecture of the forest has resulted from a sort of tug-of-war between the need to absorb water and nutrients from the earth below while competing with neighboring plants for the light coming from the sun above. The elevated canopy came into being as competing plants evolved different ways of reaching above each other. Even though the tropics are bathed in almost twice as much sun as regions at the latitude of Paris, there never seems to be enough to go around.

Evolution has solved this dilemma in several ways. The most straightforward is the tree trunk. The forest giants, such as the Brazil nut tree, rise twenty stories or more, hoisting their foliage above the main mass of the canopy. In these enormous trees, water and nutrients are pulled up through the trunks by the vacuum created as water evaporates from the surface of leaves far above; the pull of the vacuum can exceed 2 to 3 tons per square inch. Farther down, in the understory, is a mixture of palms and slimmer trees that tolerate perpetual twilight. There are palms on stilts, palms covered with spines, palms that climb like vines, palms with berries, and palms with nuts. And the forest floor is covered with saplings and seedlings that remain stunted until some tall neighbor comes crashing down and allows a flood of sunlight to pour onto the plants below.

The large trees expend an enormous amount of their productive energy in getting their green leaves as high as possible. Other plants have different strategies: climbing or perching. Myriad epiphytes – air plants – grow high in the canopy, their dust-fine seeds having lodged in the crooks of tree branches. They include ferns, orchids, peppers, and even cacti. The epiphytes are not parasites; they derive their nutrients from the rainwater coursing down the tree trunks to which they cling. Normally, rainwater alone contains insufficient nutrients to nourish a plant. But in the rain forest, as the rain splashes onto a leaf or dribbles down a stem, it absorbs organic and inorganic compounds from the surfaces of the plants or from excrement deposited by the many animal residents of the canopy. Thus, by the time a raindrop reaches one of the suspended epiphytes, it may have concentrations of nutrients such as nitrogen, phosphorus, and potassium that are anywhere from fifteen to sixty-five times higher than in normal rainwater. Some epiphytes – particularly the bromeliads, relatives of the pineapple – have evolved fleshy, waxy leaves that form a rosette which catches rainwater and organic debris that falls from the tree crowns farther up. Some of these reservoirs can hold as much as 10 gallons of water. These living cisterns have in turn become a home for frogs – and there are species that live only in certain bromeliads.

Other plants, such as the lianas that form an impassible tangle in parts of the Amazon, use larger trees as a ladder on which they climb toward the sun. Some of these coiled vines would measure up to 3,000 feet if straightened out. They have evolved some intricate strategies for reaching the sunlit heights. A botanist named Tom Ray studied the climbing behavior of a vine species with the ghoulish name *Monstera gigantea*; he found that as a seedling, this vine initially grows toward the *darkest* place within reach. Most of the time, the darkest spot in the forest is the base of the largest tree. Once the vine finds a tree, somehow it changes strategies and begins to seek sunlight.

Then there are the true parasitic plants, such as the strangler fig, which begins its life as an epiphyte high in the canopy where it first lodged as a seed excreted by a bird or monkey. The young plant unreels long, thin roots that resemble dangling bungee cords and spreads its parasol of leaves to catch the sun. If a root touches down in a spot relatively rich in leaf litter, the plant begins to thrive as nutrients get pumped up the roots. Quickly, more roots descend. Over a period of years, the thickening mass of dangling roots begins to fuse and can eventually completely encase the host tree, as if it had been dipped in cement. The mummified host dies and rots, providing a rich source of nutrients for the fig, which has made the transition from something you might see hanging in a macramé sling in a garden shop into a massive, 150-foot-tall giant.

To anyone from a temperate latitude, it is a bit startling to learn that a veteran tropical botanist can come upon an Amazonian tree and matter-of-factly state that he does not know its species. Yet it happens all the time, and it is a testament to the diversity of living things in a rain forest that such confusion still reigns.

© 1990 by Andrew Revkin. Adapted from the book *The Burning Season*, published by Houghton Mifflin.

1990

J. F. W. Gourlay
["Reforestation"]

In the 1850s, at the same time as the great attack on the pine forests of Ontario, pioneers settled Ontario's agricultural land. Settlers followed the loggers into the Ottawa Valley and into the rest of southern Ontario. Early pioneer families saw the forest as an obstacle. To farm the land and grow enough food to survive, each family cleared about two hectares per year.

However, even at this time, a number of notable people were concerned about the destruction of forests for settling land. The Select Committee, headed by James Burke, reported to the government in 1854 that: "practical men ... realized the desirability of maintaining timber in the non-agricultural regions...."

The report made people aware that perhaps trees should be planted to protect the land from erosion. Wildfires were also a severe problem and people thought that protecting forests for wood was also important.

However, it took 17 years to focus attention on reforestation and the need to protect forested lands in general. In 1871, the Ontario legislature passed an act that encouraged landowners to plant trees next to provincial roads. It appears that the government took the first step towards this first partnership.

In 1883, the *Ontario Tree Planting Act* built upon the success of the 1871 Act, and there are still several treed areas growing across the province that were planted as a result of this act.

From "The Partnership Continues," *Your Forests,* Silver Anniversary
Issue 1966-1991.
Source: (Publication copied from) Ministry of Natural Resources.
Copyright: 1991 Queen's Printer Ontario.

1991

Adam Thorpe
[From tree to furniture]

He could spot a tree as were ready better nor arn other. That was what he had. Dead o' winter, frost cracklin, sap down, first light up in the copses – Baylee mainly, good oak there, middlin tough acause the soil en't thin, an Smithy Copse for elm, an top o' Frum Down for beech, though they've mostly gone now, them as were past Five Elms Farm, on account o' the storms, for they don't root deep, beech, an they were right on brow there, afore sarsens, though there be a fine clump on the estate, agin river, where they put that daft temple, aye, an wych astraddle the river ater Quabb Bottom just afore old Master Pottinger's mill, goin up, in Grigg's, for we needed a goodish lot o' wych, for the furniture, though I prefers the Dutch, plenty o' that out Bursop way, an roundabouts, Dutch bein easy on the palm an works wi' you, don't it? – an there he'd be, deep in Baylee, eyein this butt, that butt, an allus better nor his bro for seein the wheel in the crooked uns, ezackerly right, an ud mark 'em, I can see him now, wi' a flick o' the gouge an stride through the old mist, cracklin over the floor – an he'd be fellin the next day, he'd be that quick at hagglin.

They'd crash down all right. He'd have the butts in the bob in no time, up there in the woods. You go to the yard now, see the elm stacked, right hand o' saw-pit, we cut down eight, nine year ago, when we were still gristy. That be my work there, though I won't never fashion it. Could tell you where ivery one of 'em stood, once. All out Bursop way. Ivery one have a tale in her. Like haaf as be fashioned out o' timber in Ulver, I can tell you where it come from, what dern tree. See that old door there? Twenty year old, but it were once up atop Basing's Down, north end o' Swilly Copse, pleasurin its leaves in grawin weather, rustlin in wind. Afore we lopped she, an one day's work got a door out.

Reprinted with the permission of Reed Books from *Ulverton*, VI, by Adam Thorpe, London, Reed Books.

1992

ɶ

Roald Hoffmann
["The growing that is life"]

I believe that our soul has an innate need for the chanced, the unique, the growing that is life. I see a fir tree trying to grow in an apparent absence of topsoil, in a cleft of a cliffside of Swedish granite near Millesgården, and I think how it, or its offspring, will eventually split that rock. The plants trying to live in my office remind me of that tree. Even the grain in the wood of my desk, though it tells me of death, tells me of that tree. I see a baby satisfied after breast feeding, and its smile unlocks a neural path to memory of the smiles of my children when they were small, to a line of ducklings forming after their mother, to that tree. As A. R. Ammons says, "My nature singing in me is your nature singing."

From *The Same and Not the Same,* by Roald Hoffmann. Copyright © 1995 by Columbia University Press. Reprinted with permission of the publisher.

1995

Drawing from the cover of the booklet Prepared For The Woods, *Ottawa, Emergency Preparedness Canada, Ministry of Supply and Services.*

1995

APPENDIX

A Brief Index of Themes and Categories

For those among us who like formal plantations with parks, order, and system, we attempt here, with the greatest diffidence, to provide an index of categories and themes, together with a sampling of three selections under each heading. The assumption is that any reader who wishes may expand the listings in each category, or, indeed, the headings themselves, to reflect personal tastes, opinions, and discoveries. The sort of classification we suggest here is very different from a scientific botanical survey and must by its very nature be somewhat arbitrary; moreover, it will be felt that some passages belong to more than one group.

It should not be surprising if the largest groupings fall under "Tropes" and "Lyrical." Is it possible that dim atavistic recollections of our primeval relationship with trees lie behind poets' frequent use of trees as a subject in their lyrics as well as writers' habitual recourse to trees in their choice of symbols, metaphors, and similes and in their construction of allegories and analogies?

A third large group will be "Nature Humanized." Since the time when human beings left off being hunter-gatherers and became farmers the interface between primeval nature and cultivation has always been, one imagines, an overriding human issue. The writers who have celebrated the taming and domesticating of the natural landscape would be represented in this category. Throughout history, however, there have been those who have taken alarm at humanity's destructiveness in the name of civilization and progress. "Nature Despoiled" would provide for the authors who stress civilization's encroachment upon the primeval forest.

Over the millennia, from "Genesis" to D. H. Lawrence, writers have portrayed trees as a part of the living nature that is either the dwelling place, the temple, or the handiwork of divinity. Hence our category: "The Sacred Grove: Nature and the Divine." In a separate grouping titled "Myth and Religion" there would be portrayals of such memorable trees as the cedars of Irnini (Ishtar), the trees of life and of knowledge in Eden, the mighty ash Ygdrasill, and Buddha's Bodhi tree. (Of course writers' sense of reverence and awe for wooded nature in its abundance and beauty does not depend on an overt association with divinity or deity. Trees in their own right may elicit the response that we would call "The Sense of Wonder.") Within nature's cycle trees, finally, like human beings, are (in Shelley's words) subject to "Time, Occasion, Chance, and Change" and hence are fitting vehicles for meditations on "Time and Timelessness," another of our categories.

Trees throughout recorded history have been written about on a spectrum ranging from the paradisal innocence of Milton's Eden through the foreboding ambivalence of George Meredith's "Woods of Westermain" to the sinister darkness of Hawthorne's forests of the night. These kinds of treatment of the theme of trees might be headed, respectively, "Arcadian Nature," "Ambivalent Nature," and "Malevolent Nature."

But writing about trees has never been the exclusive prerogative of poets. The common people have written about trees in mnemonic rhymes on the seasons and the weather, in verse for school primers, and in popular songs and tales. These kinds of writing might be classified as "The Folk and Trees." Moreover, throughout recorded history writers have celebrated the multifarious uses that trees may be put to by human beings. Such treatments might come under the heading "Serviceable Nature." And, finally, the seemingly mundane topic "Woodsmen and Woodcraft" can be memorably treated by such diverse writers as Homer, Disraeli, D. H. Lawrence, and Alice Munro.

A list of these and other categories follows below.

Ambivalent Nature: William Cowper, "The Shrubbery," ca. 1781; George Meredith, ["Enter these enchanted woods"], 1883; Joseph Conrad, ["Wanderers on prehistoric earth"], 1899.

Arcadian Nature: William Shakespeare, ["Sweet are the uses of adversity"], 1600; Alexander Pope, ["Order in variety"], 1713; Mark Twain, ["At the farm"], 1898.

Eloquent/Picturesque: *Beowulf*, [Grendel's mere], ca. 8th century; James Fenimore Cooper, ["The vastness of the view"], 1840; William Faulkner, ["Brooding and inscrutable impenetrability"], 1942.

Fancy/Fantasy: Ovid, [Phoebus Apollo and Daphne], ca. 5 B.C.; Thomas Nashe, [Rome], 1594; Earle Birney, "From the Hazel Bough," 1945-1947.

The Folk and Trees: Anonymous, ["My little nut tree"], 16th or 17th century; Anonymous, [Oak and ash], ca. 1700; Anonymous, ["Beware"], ca. 1700.

Humour: Anonymous, [The twelve days of Christmas], ca. 18th century; Edward Lear, ["There was an old man in a tree"], ca. 1846; Ogden Nash, "Song of the Open Road," ca. 1932.

Joy of Trees: Li Po, "A Summer Day," 8th century; Robert Frost, "Birches," 1914; Roy Campbell, "Autumn," 1930.

Lyrical: Robert Burns, "Their Groves o' Sweet Myrtle," 1795; Walt Whitman, "I Saw in Louisiana a Live-Oak Growing," 1855; W.B. Yeats, ["O chestnut tree..."], 1926.

Malevolent Nature: Dante, [The dark wood], ca. 1315; Edmund Spenser, ["Wandering to and fro in ways unknown"], 1589; Nathaniel Hawthorne, ["The haunted forest"], 1835.

Myth and Religion: *Gilgamesh*, [The Cedar Mountain of the Gods], ca. 2000 B.C.; The Bible, ["A garden eastward in Eden"], ca. 1000 B.C.; Thomas Bulfinch, [Ygdrasill], 1855.

Nature Despoiled: Jane Austen, [Improvements], 1814; Gerard Manley Hopkins, "Binsey Poplars," 1879; George Sturt, ["The death of Old England"], 1923.

Nature Humanized: Elizabeth Barrett Browning, ["A sweet familiar nature"], 1857; Evelyn Waugh, ["Two realities and two dreams"], 1944; Margaret Laurence, ["That house in Manawaka"], 1963.

Pathetic Fallacy: Joseph Conrad, ["Wanderers on a prehistoric earth"], 1899; Charles G. D. Roberts, "The Solitary Woodsman," 1898; Philip Larkin, "The Trees," 1974.

Plain Prose: William Cobbett, [The oak on Tilford Green], 1822; James
W. Wells, [The Brazilian forest], 1886; Ernest Hemingway, [Nick falls
asleep], 1925.

The Sacred Grove: Nature and the Divine: John Milton, [A view of
Eden], 1674; Sir James George Frazer, ["A strange and recurring
tragedy"], 1890; Daisaku Ikeda, [The Buddha and the Bodhi tree],
1973.

The Sense of Wonder: Henry Thoreau, ["The shrines I visited"], 1854; D.
H. Lawrence, ["The deep sensual soul"], ca. 1920; John Fowles,
[Wistman's Wood], 1979.

Serviceable Nature: John Evelyn, "Of the Hasel," 1679; William Byrd,
["The pines in this part of the country"], 1728; Anonymous,
"Fireplace Logs," 1974.

Time and Timelessness: A. E. Housman, ["On Wenlock Edge"], 1896;
Thomas Hardy, "At Day-Close in November," 1914; Philip Larkin,
["Time"], 1945.

Tropes: Trees as Vehicle: George Wither, "The Palm," 1635; Robert
Southey, "The Holly Tree," 1798; Edward Thomas, "Lights Out," 1916.

Vital Nature: William Wordsworth, "Nutting," 1798; W. H. Hudson,
["That leafy cloudland"], 1904; Emily Carr, ["Green"], 1946.

Woodsmen and Woodcraft: Ernest Thompson Seton, "Sam's Woodcraft
Exploit," 1903; Thomas Hardy, "Throwing a Tree," 1928; Alice Munro,
[Woodcraft], 1980.

Index